BEYOND HONEY

BEYOND HONEY

Enjoy the magic of the bees!

[signature]

TIERNEY MONAHAN

NEW DEGREE PRESS

COPYRIGHT © 2021 TIERNEY MONAHAN

All rights reserved.

BEYOND HONEY

ISBN 978-1-63730-451-8 *Paperback*
    978-1-63730-559-1 *Kindle Ebook*
    978-1-63730-560-7 *Ebook*

To Mom and Pop

Contents

Introduction

What weighs less than a button yet contributes nearly $20 billion to the crop production industry?

The honey bee.

For many people, honey bees are simply creatures that sting you or are a nuisance when you are enjoying the pool on a hot summer day. They are tiny insects that are insignificant, aggressive, and should be killed if they fly too close. These are common thoughts.

Ancient traditions, however, talk about the meaning of bees as symbols of honesty, unity, community, strength, diligence, and vigilance.

To me, honey bees are teachers and friends—wise creatures that can educate us about ourselves and the world. My bees helped me to find connection with other people and meaning in my small, daily tasks. I have surrendered more peacefully to washing the dishes or analyzing a spreadsheet, and become more open to collaboration with others, even if it is imperfect.

Our world is hurting. The environment is suffering unparalleled damage at the hands of humans. There is a greater than 95 percent probability that the current warming trend of planet Earth is due to human activity since the mid-twentieth century (NASA 2021). Global temperature rise, warming oceans, shrinking glaciers, sea level rise, and extreme weather events are many of the problems we are facing today, and will continue to face in the coming years.

In the West, we have glorified individualism and self-sufficiency. We imagine ourselves as immune to the influence of others while we pursue our destiny. Studies suggest that we are shaped by our social environment, and we suffer greatly when social bonds are threatened or severed (Cook 2013). There is a loneliness epidemic that is rippling across the globe. One in four Americans rarely or never feel as though there are people who understand them, and only 50 percent of Americans have meaningful, in-person social interactions with friends or family each day (Collins 2018).

This is where honey bees can offer their sage example. By using their exemplary model of "willing the good of the other more than their own good," bees teach us to be less selfish and more attuned to the needs of those around us. They show us that knowing your role leads to harmony and equilibrium as each bee completes the task for which it has been made. This can empower us to move forward knowing that our daily tasks are not just chores to be done as quickly as possible, but in the ordinariness of what we are called to do lies the road to fulfillment.

Facing the reality of our actions, we must strive to collaborate on solutions to our most pressing challenges. Of course, there are leaders and guides who may shepherd the work. But, most often, they are part of a team or family that supports their efforts.

Honey bees depend on one another for their survival.

No honey bee can go it alone.

As humans, we too, need others not just to survive, but to thrive. We are made for conversation and touch. We need connection. In fact, not only do we need it, but we are designed for it—we are "wired" to connect.

My dearest friends will tell you that I am always seeking to deepen my connection—connection with myself, connection with others, connection with nature, and connection with God. I see all this seeking and striving as never-ending; a desire that will be with me until the end of my days.

My hope of hopes is that, by the end of this book, you will become a friend to the bees. In the chapters that follow, I will explore the environmental, economic, and entrepreneurial impact of honey bees on our society through research and real-life stories. Pause, take a deep breath, and welcome the wisdom of the bees.

PART ONE

CHAPTER 1

Bees as Teachers

If you grew up learning about Jane Goodall, you know that animals can transform our lives simply by being themselves.

In the documentary *My Octopus Teacher*, Craig Foster follows an octopus for one year, visiting her in the ocean every day off the coast of South Africa (Foster 2020). After a difficult day in which a pyjama shark bit off one of the octopus' legs, Foster realized how much the incident had affected him. He said, "I realized I was changing; she was teaching me to become sensitized to the other—especially wild creatures" (Foster 2020). Despite thousands of years of studying animals, there is still so much mystery about the inner workings of these creatures. We can observe and study and imagine the "why" of their actions, but, in the end, there is still a lot that is up for interpretation.

When I was a little girl, I spent hours and hours exploring our backyard and our neighborhood, observing plants and animals.

I was more carefree as a child than I am now as an adult.

I have a photo of myself playing softball in middle school in which I am gazing out on the world, contemplating. I think that is one of the truest parts about me—the contemplative, the meditative, the thoughtful. I have always thought and observed more than I have talked. Yes, I was that child burning with existential curiosity and ruminating about the meaning of life and death.

Now, if I pass by a flower with a bee or an insect on it, I usually stop, even for a few seconds, and admire how gentle they are in their movements. They are so subtle, lightly flying or walking. What would happen if we all took a few seconds to observe nature each day? Would it change us?

I noticed that when I began working with honey bees as an adult, some of those same emotions that I felt as a child returned to me. Almost as if I came home to myself. To my kinder, gentler, slower-moving self.

I am only now seeing my sensitivity as my superpower—not as something to be fixed, but as something to be embraced. I am a deep processor and need time to reflect and think. Nature allows me the time to ponder and muse about life. It also helps me to reacquaint myself with myself—to recognize my inner voice instead of listening to the noise.

LESSONS FROM THE ANIMAL KINGDOM

Animals can teach us compassion or fierce protection. They can be solitary, or they can thrive in packs. Each animal has its own lesson to teach us.

Humans (*Homo sapiens*) and honey bees (*Apis mellifera*) are two very different beings. Honey bees are a creature that can be found in laboratories across the world. Entomologists have studied this tiny creature, and many other bee species, trying to uncover the reason behind certain behaviors. The study of bees, known as melittology, helps us to understand the environment and our interactions within our greater ecosystem. Honey bees are social creatures. The study of honey bees, known as apiology, is an important field of study that allows humans to tackle questions on the evolution of social systems.

The survival of both honey bees and other species of bees is critical to our survival as humans. Native bees, like mason bees and leafcutter bees, as well as bumble bees, are vital for pollination. There are over 20,000 species of bees! The honey bee impacts our lives not only because it pollinates our food, but in working with bees, we can also become more attuned with nature and with ourselves.

In her book, *The Truth About Animals*, Lucy Cooke explains, "When seeking to understand animals, context is key. We have a habit of viewing the animal kingdom through the prism of our own, rather narrow, existence" (Cooke 2018). Unraveling the myths surrounding honey bees is one feat. Convincing people to change their minds is another.

In particular, we keep bees for pollination services. They serve our end goal of pollinating the fruits, vegetables, and nuts we eat to survive. Our diet would be remarkably less diverse without them. We would lose almonds, apples, blueberries, cherries, cranberries, kiwi, macadamia nuts, mangos, melons, pumpkins, squash, and many more.

There are striking photos of what the grocery store would look like without bees: the produce section has entire shelves and display cases that are empty. If you type it into your search bar, you can see for yourself what I am talking about—it is quite shocking. We sometimes use these images in educational workshops to build awareness about how important these creatures are to our daily sustenance.

As life becomes more precarious for the honey bee due to climate change, pesticides, disease, and habitat loss, it is a warning for us humans. If life is untenable for the honey bee, it means that it is becoming untenable for other species and may become untenable for us as humans.

HAPPENINGS IN THE HIVE

A honey bee colony is comprised of three types of members: the queen bee, worker bees, and drone bees. For each colony, there is one queen bee. The queen bee becomes a queen by being fed royal jelly in the larval stage. I will discuss royal jelly in more depth in a future chapter. The worker bees, the females, are the heart of the hive. They perform many daily tasks to keep the hive running smoothly, including feeding the baby brood, cleaning the hive, protecting the queen, foraging for food, etc. The drone bees, the males, have only one purpose: to mate with the queen. Typically, drone bees will not mate with the queen that is in their own hive; they will mate with another queen in drone congregation zones while flying.

When working within the hive, honey bees are some of the most cooperative animals on the planet. Everything they do is in service of the queen and their fellow bees. They tend to each other's needs, without second-guessing.

When beekeepers are responsible for managed hives, the primary tasks they perform are to aid the colony in anything it may be lacking, including providing supplementary food. During a hive inspection, a beekeeper will take wooden frames out of the hive (if using a woodenware system) and carefully look for signs of activity or problems. Healthy hives will have adequate amounts of brood (baby bees), pollen, and honey. The brood replace any sick or dead members and contribute to building-up the colony to fight off disease and predators. Pollen and honey are the food resources that need to be well-stocked, especially as a hive enters the winter season.

SEASONS OF THE BEES

In spring, the bees emerge from the hive after a long winter. Their priorities shift from survival mode to building-up the hive's resources, which includes brood, pollen, and honey. The queen will begin to lay 1–2,000 eggs per day. If there is no sign of eggs or young brood, the queen will need to be replaced.

For the beekeeper, spring is the time to replace hives that have died and to troubleshoot underperforming hives. This may be the time to replace the queen, order new colonies, or combine a weaker colony with a stronger colony. The beekeeper may choose to feed the colony a sugar syrup mixture if they do not appear to have enough food. Beekeepers need to keep an eye on pest level and may choose to treat the hive with a miticide to reduce the chances of an overpowering mite problem.

Colonies may swarm and, in that case, they will look for a new home. Beekeepers may reduce the chance of swarming by creating "splits," essentially splitting the hive in half, and adding a new queen to one of the remaining half-colonies. Beekeepers can also keep empty boxes to attract potential swarms, either from their own colony or other neighboring colonies.

In summer, the bees continue to build up the pollen and honey storage to prepare for the autumn and winter months. This is the time a beekeeper may add more woodenware boxes and frames to capture more honey stores. Checks for pesticide levels continue throughout the year, including during the summer. Other flying insects like yellow jackets or hornets may be attracted to the hive and try to rob the colony of its food stores.

Honey is harvested during the summer months. The beekeeper should leave approximately 40–50 pounds of honey per colony to ensure the hive has enough stores for the approaching autumn and winter months. If there is a dearth and no nectar is to be found and the bees have eaten through their storage, the beekeeper may choose to feed the colony supplemental sugar syrup. The beekeeper must also ensure that there are enough water sources in the flying range of the bees.

In autumn, the bees are starting to venture out less and less as the temperatures drop. A beekeeper may choose to add a quilt box to prevent moisture or improve insulation (if they are in particularly cold climates). This is also the time to add a mouse guard and to close openings to the smallest size entrance to prevent unwelcome visitors.

In winter, the bees are huddling together in a tight cluster to maintain warmth. They typically do not leave the hive unless the temperatures rise to unseasonable highs. Even then, the flights are mostly for cleansing (releasing waste) rather than foraging. Beekeepers do not generally open the hives, except to add sugar fondant cakes (the winter alternative to sugar syrup) if the food stores are running low.

During the winter, the beekeeper will generally order, assemble, repair, and paint equipment to prepare for spring. This is also the time to think ahead and place pre-orders for packages of bees, nucleus colonies, and queens, which will replace any sick or dead colonies that did not survive the winter.

WHAT CAN WE LEARN FROM HONEY BEES?

For this book, I conducted interviews for several months to hear how honey bees are impacting people in their everyday lives. I also asked people their favorite characteristics of the honey bee, and what honey bees could teach us. I received varying responses: "work ethic" (Mark Dykes, extension and Bee Squad coordinator for the vanEngelsdorp Bee Lab at the University of Maryland), "willingness to serve" and "resilience" (Ginger and Daniel Fenwick, Bees4Vets), "understanding their role" (Steve Jimenez, Hives for Heroes), and "their sense of a greater good" (Paige Mulhern, The Best Bees Company).

Honey bees work hard, regardless of what is happening inside or outside the hive. They never quit. They are always looking for the next opportunity to serve the good of the hive. For example, if the honeycomb is damaged in the process of a human inspecting a hive, the bees will rush to repair it.

In my conversation with Mark Dykes, we discussed honey bees and their characteristics. I have had the pleasure of hearing Mark speak on several occasions and have attended some of the Bee Squad educational webinars, as I am always eager to learn more about bees. He was very warm and personable and offered so many nuggets of wisdom during our interview. "From basically the minute they are born, or emerge, to the time they die, they are working. All decisions are made to help benefit the whole, not the individual," said Mark. "Bees are very altruistic, they're very good decision-makers."

Inside the hive, honey bees are not competitive. They are driven by the mission to sustain the colony and they work together to achieve what is best for the hive. A honey bee knows when another bee is in distress and comes to its aid. Honey bees communicate information about where to find the best plants for foraging through a "waggle dance." The dance directs the other forager bees to know where they can collect more food for their hive to grow.

Bees keep each other informed about changes in the environment and pass along information they receive to others. Their community is efficient, harmonious, and unified.

The way humans move about in the world is often driven by our own interests, needs, and wants. Many cultures are steeped in individualism. Relying on other people is often looked down upon. Becoming independent and self-sufficient is seen as an ultimate good. However, the truth is that we need each other. We cannot do everything alone. We typically buy food and clothes made by other peoples' hands, for example. Even if we live alone and support ourselves financially, there are parts of our lives that will inevitably overlap with others.

Throughout their life cycle, worker bees will hold several jobs: brood raiser, honeycomb builder, pollen packer, hive repairer, queen cleaner, food forager, etc. They do their jobs and they do them well. Each bee abides by what it has been called to do at that specific time in its life. They synchronize all tasks. Honey bees do not multi-task, but work on the task that they are most capable of doing, focusing on that top priority.

They do not drain their energy by "biting off more than they can chew." As humans, we switch jobs, careers, and even tasks quite often. I am not saying that we should stay in the same job forever, but we can learn a lot from focusing on the task at hand and honing our skills to concentrate on what we are called to do in the moment, rather than being bogged down by past or future worries.

As beekeepers, we inspect the hives every week. We manipulate their environment by taking out frames (removing the wooden frames from the box), cutting out burr comb (this extra comb produced by bees outside of the frames needs to be periodically removed so that the hive can still be opened), and adding or removing honey supers (boxes that the bees have filled with honey). Honey bees always manage to overcome these changes.

They also resist pests and invaders by working together to ward off the enemies, blocking the entrance to the hive, or cornering them with no chance to escape. They take what comes at them and they keep moving forward. Honey bees have survived for centuries, despite facing challenge after challenge.

Bees are incredibly adaptive and may even take on a task that is not specifically "theirs," but in the absence of another bee suited to the task, they will do it. Honey bees will shift responsibilities when necessary to accomplish the goals for the hive. They ensure that the collective productivity of the hive as a whole is not lost.

If the hive is moved or they are relocated, they will work to understand their new environment. They do not become discouraged by cold or hot weather, they simply huddle together for warmth or fan their wings to cool down the hive, depending on which end of the spectrum they find the temperature.

If a honey bee is sick, it will often fly away or leave the hive to die alone, choosing to sacrifice itself rather than potentially infecting the whole hive with disease. Even when a bee stings someone or something and sacrifices herself, she is doing it to protect the hive.

Honey bees do not eat just for their own nutrition. When they take in food, they are sharing it with the other bees in the hive. It is a communal stomach. Honey bees will collect nectar for the hive, knowing full well that they will not be alive to see the final product: honey. The forager who collects the nectar is at the end of its life cycle and will never taste the sweetness of her labor, for she will die before the honey is ready.

Honey bees work for the greater good, not for their individual advancement. Of course, many human beings are generous; however, many are also greedy. The "I want it and I want it now" mentality is non-existent in the hive.

Drawing connections between humans and honey bees will be flawed and imperfect. However, there is value in observing animals in nature, learning from them, and becoming the best versions of ourselves. Returning to the wisdom of Lucy Cooke in *The Truth About Animals*, she mentions, "... we have a history of viewing the rest of the animal kingdom as simply here to service our needs. This selfish standpoint has resulted in many of our most misguided mistakes. In these times of mass extinction, we cannot afford to make many more" (Cooke 2018).

We need to think more critically about the relationship between animals and humans, and act decisively with compassion and an instinct to preserve and enhance the relationship, rather than from a mentality of "you are only valuable to me if you are useful to me." If honey bees die, our own inevitable demise will follow thereafter. Listening to the bees, learning from them as teachers, can show us the way forward.

CHAPTER 2

Interdependence

What does beekeeping have to do with how we depend on each other?

I have benefited from working outside in the sunshine, collaborating with the natural world and other beekeepers, and learning from the earth. It helps me to remember that I am just one of many creatures on Earth and puts me in a position to receive from the world. By working in cooperation with numerous and varied beings, I am less likely to force or grasp for something that is not truly mine to own. Reciprocity with nature is a beautiful ideal that we often fail to practice.

When I am working with the bees, I can tune out my worries—it is calming and centering. As I concentrate on the task at hand, their buzzing creates almost a meditative experience. I deal with anxiety, depression, and chronic illness, and beekeeping has been one activity that has provided relief in my daily fight forward toward a whole, joyful life.

How did I get here?

I happened upon beekeeping during my research about gardening in the hopes of increasing the yield of my vegetables. I did not seriously think of pursuing it until I had a garden and a yard of my own. Unfortunately, I was placed on the waiting list the first year that I tried to enroll in a beginner's class. Luckily, the second year I was successful, and was trained as a beekeeper in the spring of 2019 through the DC Beekeepers Alliance course, in partnership with the University of the District of Columbia. It opened my eyes to a whole new part of the ecosystem that I had never explored in depth.

I am fascinated by this tiny creature who has such a huge impact on the world—on our food systems and pollination services, on biodiversity and the environment, and even in improving economic livelihoods and prompting entrepreneurial ventures.

Bees and beekeeping can be transformative for economic revitalization. Bees are not only fascinating creatures to observe, but they also have a hand in bringing people together. Due to the many positive qualities of honey bees and working with bees, transformational training programs have been founded over the last few decades. These programs have worked with former miners, incarcerated persons, those reintegrating back into society, veterans, first responders, and rural farms in emerging markets.

Bees and beekeeping have also provided opportunities for creative entrepreneurship, mostly arising in urban areas. Abandoned lots have been transformed into pollinator gardens. Beehives are being rented and managed on high-rise rooftops. Companies have harnessed the medicinal benefits of beehive resources (honey, propolis, royal jelly, and pollen) to create wellness and wound healing products.

Bees and their hives are a microcosm of the world, and they offer a mirror for us humans. They can show us how the planet is doing and if we are bringing harm to the world through our actions. If the bees are doing poorly, it often means the entire ecosystem is struggling. Their attunement to the environment allows them to be a barometer for environmental health.

CURRENT STATE

The Bee-Apocalypse. Bye Bye Bees. Headlines swept across the world in 2006 when there were catastrophic, unexplained losses of honey bee colonies. Fifteen years later, yes, honey bees still need our help.

The relationship between bees and humans is one of interdependence. We depend on bees to pollinate the food we eat and, in turn, must practice efforts to provide pollinators with proper forage and habitats (or, rather, we should do our best to avoid harming bees further through our human activities that damage plants and the environment). There is a web of interdependency within our ecosystem between microbes, fungi, plants, and animals.

Honey bees experience multiple stressors that cause an increase in colony mortality. Solutions must consider the various causes and their interactions. As stated in a 2016 study by Moritz and Erler, "The past decade has seen a multitude of dramatic reports on honey bee declines that raised great public and societal concern. Indeed, the value of the honey bees for human society has been estimated to exceed 153 billion primarily as key pollinators of many crops" (Moritz and Erler 2016). For example, the honey bee is crucial for commercial pollination of almond crops in California.

No honey bees, no almonds.

Further, "a global decline of honey bee colonies would be of particular concern because of large-scale declines in wild pollinators and a global loss of pollinators would clearly have profound and devastating impact on life on Earth, a sinister scenario that sparked a huge debate in the public media" (Moritz and Erler 2016). I am primarily focusing on honey bees since those are the bees that I have worked with and interacted with over the last few years. However, I would be remiss if I did not point out that other pollinators, such as native bees, caterpillars, butterflies, bats, and birds, are extremely important to the functioning of our ecosystem and need to be protected and cared for just as much, if not more, than honey bees.

COLONY COLLAPSE DISORDER

Thankfully, honey bees are no longer experiencing the dreaded Colony Collapse Disorder (CCD), a term coined in 2006. *Merriam-Webster* defines CCD as "a disorder of honeybees (*Apis mellifera*) that is of unknown cause and that is characterized by sudden colony death due to the disappearance of all adult worker bees in a hive while immature bees, the queen bee, and the honey remain" (Merriam-Webster 2021).

I have unfortunately experienced colony loss. This happened in my first year of beekeeping, due to a combination of two pests: Varroa mites and wax moths. One colony (let us call it the "gray" colony due to its external paint color) had been weak from the start, and my inexperience caused me to keep feeding it resources, rather than replacing the queen or merging the gray colony with my other colony, the "blue" colony.

Regardless, I plowed ahead, even using miticide (twice!), and the gray colony still collapsed. It was devastating. My mom was in town for a visit, and we drove out to see the hives which were hosted on my friend's farm, Stohlman Acres. I had a bad feeling when I did not see any bees flying in and out of the entrance.

I opened the gray hive, and the smell was overpowering. Thousands of bees were lying dead inside, fermenting in the hot summer sun. I started to cry, a full-blown mess under my bee suit—tears and sweat mixing together. I felt like I had failed the bees. I had let them down, done something wrong, or not done enough things right.

It was then that I knew I was connected to the bees. They had a profound effect on me, and my relationship with them was not one-sided. I had formed a bond with them, so much so that their loss was felt keenly and profoundly in my heart. I am glad that my mom was with me that day because I do not know if I would have had the stamina to clean up the hive by myself.

The question is, what causes the loss?

The varying aspects that affect honey bees include: "pathogens, pesticides, and their interactions, but also climate change, landscape alteration, agricultural intensification and non-native species" (Moritz and Erler 2016).

Unfortunately, there is still no definitive answer to the mystery of Colony Collapse Disorder (CCD). "In spite of considerable research efforts CCD could not be clearly associated with a specific pathogen or poisoning. As a consequence, interactions among pests, pathogens and pesticides were suspected to have caused these massive colony deaths" (Moritz and Erler 2016). The most reasonable conclusion has been that it was caused by an interaction of these multiple factors, a cocktail of bugs, diseases, chemicals, and unsuitable habitats, etc.

I want to return to my conversation with Mark Dykes as he mentioned that the news surrounding Colony Collapse Disorder highlighted the issue and the plight of the honey bee. However, it also heightened the drama and created misconceptions surrounding what was termed the "Bee-Apocalypse." He said, "We understand there are problems, we still see huge losses each year. If a cattle farmer lost 40 percent of their herd each year they'd be out of business in a year."

He mentioned that due to the high percentage of losses, his concern is that beekeepers will go extinct since it will not be financially viable for people to keep bees. "If you're making up the losses that you're having every year, if we cross 40–50 percent average annual loss, it is going to be hard." Of course, the health of the honey bees is important to stave off any further loss. "By coming up with the best management practices that can reduce losses through other means—through non-chemical means, through husbandry, through cultural practices—those are the types of things that will ultimately help save the industries," Mark concluded.

While we are no longer dealing with the tragic losses from CCD, we still need to tackle each of these factors in a way that takes into account their interactive nature. We cannot target only one factor (for example, pests) and expect colonies to thrive.

INTERDEPENDENCE

As Mark explained, we must support beekeeping and beekeepers. "It is the decline in beekeeping activity and the increase of honey trade that is of concern. A global honey market with low honey prices in exporting countries may make it less attractive for professional beekeepers in importing countries to produce honey with their own colonies" (Moritz and Erler 2016).

Honey bees are important for more reasons than just the honey they produce; however, it is the compensation through honey sales and colony sales that allows beekeepers to continue working and turning a profit. If the price of honey is so low and the cost of beekeeping is so high, the number of beekeepers will dwindle as the benefits do not outweigh the costs.

I know that I lost money in my first year of beekeeping.

I invested in all the equipment and woodenware boxes, and I purchased two nucleus colonies. Since one colony died and one absconded, there was no path for me to split my hives in the spring and I was faced with the cost of replacement hives—another two nucleus colonies. Thankfully, beekeeping is not my full-time job, therefore, I was financially able to accept the impact of that loss. However, I can imagine the real anxiety that full-time beekeepers experience each summer and winter as they wait to see if their colonies will survive through the two toughest periods of the year.

"Honey bee colonies are typically lost over winter, and this places the beekeeper into a pivotal position for honey bee conservation" (Moritz and Erler 2016). Beekeepers play a role in the continuation of the species through the replacement of lost hives, typically from another beekeeper who successfully overwintered their hives and now needs to split the colony to prevent swarming.

The consequences of a decline in apiculture are troubling: "If the linear colony declines of the past 50 years in countries like the United States, Germany, Austria, and Switzerland continue at the current pace, in the following decades it may well fall below levels where we can only hope that wild bee pollinators, other than honey bees, can provide sufficient pollination services" (Moritz and Erler 2016).

The real question is, if honey bee pollination disappears, will native pollinators be able to bear the full burden of pollination throughout the world? I fear that the answer is no. We need to support both honey bees and native bees—both serve humans and contribute to the health of the whole ecosystem.

CHAPTER 3

Our Common Home

"Bees are our canary. They are telling us through [their] deaths that there is a problem with our agricultural system," Gard Otis explained in his TEDx Talk at the University of Guelph, "It is our job to listen to them, [and] work with them" (Otis 2013). As Andrew Barron, a neuroethologist, stated in a *Time* article about Slovenian beekeeping, "Bees hold our ecologies together" (Godin 2020). I loved these images: bees as our canary in the coal mine and bees holding our ecologies together, linking their tiny bodies in a global embrace.

Human involvement affects bees, in both negative and positive ways.

Over the years, we have seen that bee pollination services help our human food supply, but pollination services also lead to the weakening of the bees' immune systems. There are trade-offs to nearly every decision. Should a chemical be sprayed to produce an unspoiled fruit which, at the same time, can adversely affect the bee's chance of survival? Should bees be trucked into California by the thousands from another region of the country to pollinate almonds, inevitably mixing bees from different colonies and potentially spreading disease?

POLLINATION

Most of the world depends on honey bees and native bees for pollination. Declines in both managed and native bee populations threaten global food security. Commercial beekeepers truck bees across the country to pollinate flowers to produce fruit, vegetables, and nuts. Honey bees can also pollinate clover and alfalfa, which feed cattle in the meat and dairy industries. Apart from human-used products, bees also pollinate plants that wild animals eat and help willows and poplars to grow, creating habitats for other species.

To prepare bees for pollination services, commercial beekeepers will feed them alternative pollen sources and sugar syrup (neither of which is as good as the nutrient-rich sources of real flowers and plants). The syrup lacks immune-boosting compounds, leaving colonies more susceptible to pathogens. Then, when bees are moved to different parts of the country for seasonal pollination, the bees tend to collect only one source of food (monocrop) in the orchard and are not foraging on a diversity of plant sources. It is like eating the same food over and over again. Imagine pizza every day, for every meal, for several weeks straight. Their immune systems, like ours, simply do better with a more diverse diet.

As we increase the large swaths of agricultural lands that are limited to one crop, the bees only consume nectar and pollen from that single source. If humans were willing to adopt other practices, including strip farming with multiple crops, the bees would be provided with multiple sources of pollen. With strip farming, a field is divided into long, narrow strips which are alternated in a crop rotation system. Including a strip of wildflowers or another flowering crop can help the bees gather nutrients for a more diverse diet. Additionally, the number of crop pests tends to go down when you intersperse different crops, which means fewer pesticides to kill those pests, leading to a reduced negative effect on the environment.

CLIMATE CHANGE AND LOSS OF HABITAT

Climate change is one of many factors affecting bees. As habitats grow warmer, places where the bees can live grow smaller, especially for native bees. There are nearly 3,600 species of native bees in North America, many of whom are solitary (Xerces Society 2018). Honey bees will seek out higher altitudes and colder temperatures, trying to regulate their bodies and hive temperatures. This also affects the circadian rhythm of the bees. Foreign bee species (like the Western honey bee which is not native to North America) are less likely to be able to adapt to these new characteristics of the environment. Unpredictable and changing seasons can impact pollen production and change the flower patterns of native plants.

Nutritional deficiency also plays a role in honey bee loss. In the United States, there has been a change in land cover as well as an increase in urbanization and the loss of cropland and natural vegetation. If bees are struggling to find adequate nutrition in the foraging radius, colony loss will be inevitable as the hives will starve to death. Honey bee nutrition depends on plants that provide both pollen and nectar. Planting native plants is one of the ways individuals can help honey bees and native bees, especially if the planting is seasonal and provides forage throughout the whole calendar year (instead of only in the spring and summer months).

There are additional environmental benefits to planting cover crops or plants beyond simply helping the honey bees including: attracting native pollinators; promoting carbon sequestration and soil health; decreasing wind and water erosion; improving water quality by intercepting sediment and nutrients; and providing good wildlife habitat for pheasant, quail, and other game species (United States Department of Agriculture 2017).

PESTICIDES

We have all heard of the dangers of pesticides. DDT ring any bells? Honey bees are reflections of ourselves. While the toll it takes on our bodies may be different, it certainly is important to pay attention to how honey bees react to pesticides. Over 150 different pesticides have been found in colony samples (Mullin et al. 2010).

The pesticides themselves can be harmful, but the misuse and improper application of pesticides can cause more damage. The misuse of pesticides can contaminate nectar, pollen, surface water, and even the dust that drifts when seeds are sown. Honey bees can travel up to three miles to forage, so it is often difficult to pinpoint where the bees are encountering pesticides within their fly radius.

Not only does exposure to pesticides impair bee behavior, but "[g]ene expression in honey bee larvae was also verified to be seriously affected by pesticide exposure. A recent work on pesticide exposure of honey bees indicated that this exposure can lead to an increased level of Nosema pathogen [disease]" (Kasiotis et al. 2014).

Beekeepers continue to work with chemical manufacturers to try and influence the formula make-up to lessen the impact on bees. Neonicotinoids, neuro-active pesticides that function similarly to nicotine, have been linked to impaired memory, movement, and death in bees. Honey bees exposed to sublethal levels of neonicotinoids can experience trouble with flight and navigation and even slower learning of new tasks, which impacts foraging abilities and hive productivity (Xerces Society 2016).

There has been progress to ban some of the large-scale spraying, but there remains the problem that growers are using seed treatments (treating the seed coat with a pesticide). Any insect that feeds on those seeds will ingest the chemical and be harmed or possibly die. There has also been an increase in exemptions that have been granted for banned neonicotinoids to combat green aphids and the virus yellows disease (insects are vectors in sugar beets). Herbicides can also reduce floral diversity.

PESTS AND PATHOGENS

During pollination services, bees can transmit mites and diseases to each other due to close contact with bees from other colonies from all over the country. If the queen becomes infected, she will transmit it to her young, the next generation. This unnatural migration leads to the spread of pathogens within their own colony and to nearby communities of native pollinators.

Other sources of pain for the honey bee are pests such as the Varroa mite (aptly named scientifically as the *Varroa destructor*), the tracheal mite (*Acarapis woodi*), the small hive beetle (*Aethina tumida*), the greater wax moth (*Galleria mellonella*), and the bee louse (*Braula coeca*).

PESTS

- Varroa Mites
  - The varroa mite is the most serious pest affecting honey bees. It is an external parasite that feeds on the blood of adult bees, larvae, and pupae.
- Tracheal Mites
  - The tracheal mite is an internal parasite that pierces the breathing tube wall of the honey bee from the inside.
- Small Hive Beetles
  - The larvae of the small hive beetle can cause damage to honeycomb, honey, and pollen by tunneling through and defecating in the hive. This activity may cause the fermentation of the honey.

- Wax Moths
    - The larvae of the greater wax moth cause damage to beeswax comb in weak or dead colonies. They also eat away at wooden surfaces and cause damage to the woodenware parts of the hive bodies.
- Bee Lice
    - The bee louse is a wingless fly that is a lesser pest. It will crawl on the adult honey bees, feeding on their mouth secretions, and will also eat honey and royal jelly.

Honey bees also suffer from brood diseases such as American foulbrood (*Histolysis infectiosa perniciosa larvae apium*, *Pestis americana larvae apium*, the causative agent is *Paenibacillus larvae*), European foulbrood *(Melissococcus pluton)*, Chalkbrood (*Ascosphaera apis*), Sacbrood, Parasitic mite syndrome (PMS), Paralysis, Nosema (*Nosema apis*), and Deformed wing virus.

PATHOGENS
- American foulbrood
    - American foulbrood (AFB) is an infectious brood disease caused by a spore-forming bacterium. It is the most widespread and destructive of brood diseases, afflicting queen, drone, and worker larvae alike. Adult bees, however, are not affected by AFB.
- European foulbrood
    - European foulbrood (EFB) is a bacterial brood disease. It is considered a stress disease and is most prevalent in spring and early summer. It is less serious than AFB, and colonies can recover from infections.

- Chalkbrood
  - Chalkbrood, a fungal brood disease of honey bees, is caused by a spore-forming fungus. Worker, drone, and queen larvae are susceptible.
- Sacbrood
  - Sacbrood, a disease caused by a virus, usually does not result in severe losses. It is most common during the first half of the brood-rearing season.
- Parasitic mite syndrome
  - This situation is associated with varroa mites, viruses, or a combination of both. Affected larvae die in the late larval or prepupal stage, stretched out in their cells often with their heads slightly raised. In the early stage of infection, they are white but dull rather than glistening, and they look deflated. These are part of a symptom complex that has been given the name "Parasitic Mite Syndrome" or PMS.
- Paralysis
  - Paralysis is a symptom of adult honey bees and is usually associated with viruses. Two different viruses, chronic bee paralysis virus (CPV) and acute bee paralysis virus (APV), have been isolated from paralytic bees. Other suspected causes of paralysis include pollen and nectar from plants such as buttercup, rhododendron, laurel, and some species of basswood; pollen deficiencies during brood-rearing in the early spring; and consumption of fermented stored pollen.
- Nosema
  - Nosema disease is caused by a spore-forming protozoan that invades the digestive tracts of honey bee

workers, queens, and drones. Nosema spores are ingested with food or water by the adult bee.

- Deformed wing virus
  - In addition, Varroa mites often carry a viral pathogen called Deformed wing virus that leads to further colony loss. The Varroa mite's original host was the Asian honey bee *(Apis cerana)* but has now expanded to the European honey bee *(Apis mellifera)*.

(Frazier 2004).

Since honey bee health is connected to the larger ecosystem, "honey bee diseases also pose risks for the wider pollinator community, and we need to understand the global drivers of disease spread in order to manage the transfer of disease to novel hosts" (Wilfert et al. 2016). If possible, the ideal would be to prevent new animals from being infected by these diseases and causing additional problems.

NATIVE POLLINATORS

Since the focus of this book is on honey bees, I do not talk about the importance of native pollinators nearly as much as I wanted to, given the narrow scope. However, it is true that managed honey bee species can negatively affect native bees. The honey bee cannot replace or make up for native pollinators. Although the vast majority of native bees do not produce honey, their real value is in their pollination power. We need native pollinators just as much, if not more than, honey bees. If we continue to only reproduce non-native species in North America

(*Apis mellifera*) and neglect the native bees, this will be detrimental in the long run.

Sweat bees, for example, are a highly efficient pollinator of many different plants. Other native bees that are important in the United States are mason bees, bumble bees, carpenter bees, miner bees, digger bees, metallic green bees, among others. In fact, many native bees are more efficient pollinators than honey bees. Honey bees only pollinate a certain number of plants (for example, they do not usually pollinate tomatoes or eggplants—native bees take care of that job).

In my conversation with Mark Dykes, he mentioned that one myth is that the honey bee is the bee that we should be saving or focusing on the most. Native bees are often lost in the shuffle as people tend to focus on saving honey bees. For native bees, habitat loss and degradation lead to the loss of nesting sites. When invasive plant species take over areas where native plants once grew, native bees may disappear from the area.

Honey bees and native bees are also important to biodiversity. They support the growth of a variety of trees, plants, and flowers that serve as shelter and wildlife habitats for other animals, as well as food for both human and non-human species. Humans negatively affect this process using herbicides to kill weeds and other plants that bees use for forage. If people adopt pollinator-friendly practices, it leads to less ecosystem degradation, including the toxic impact of chemicals. Pollinators help plants to survive. There are far reaching effects of plant survival including keeping waterways clean, preventing soil erosion, producing the oxygen we breathe, and absorbing carbon dioxide thereby counteracting global climate change.

ECOLOGICAL SOLUTIONS

Bees need more friends than keepers. We do not all need to become beekeepers, but there are practices that we can modify or replace that are friendlier to pollinators. We can plant native species (for example, choosing a succession of flowers that bloom both early and late in the season to maintain forage possibilities) and provide bees with a water source. Planting good forage, like wildflower patches and native shrubs alongside crops or highways can be beneficial. Supporting local parks and, on a smaller scale, encouraging residents to plant a wildflower mix can do wonders.

The green grass may look neat and tidy, but it does nothing to help pollinators. I recognize that people may live in communities with strict regulations about their lawn type and quality; however, if you have more freedom to plant pollinator-friendly species, I encourage you to do so. For homeowners with restrictions or apartment dwellers, even having a few potted or container plants with cosmos, lavender, lantana, sage, or thyme can be beneficial. Strict regulations can also be contested and changed by concerned citizens by proving that the harms outweigh the benefits—an opportunity to become involved in pollinator activism.

Honey bees teach us so much about how to live in a social environment and how to live a more balanced life with our environment. In working to find solutions to the world's challenges in the agricultural space (including climate change, pollution, just wages, fair labor, etc.), there needs to be an understanding of who we are as humans on the planet and how we interact with the natural world. There is room to think about mission, values, and how our careers can promote the common good. It is possible to create a profit and have a positive impact on both the planet and people.

Working for the good of the planet also means taking care of fellow humans. Our actions are not performed in isolation; there is a ripple effect on each other and our earth. We must slow down to let Earth breathe. It is important to practice proper stewardship of the atmosphere, forests, oceans, land, natural resources, and all ecosystems.

We depend on nature for our very existence, and it composes the founding elements of our society (soil, raw materials, water). We have a role in preserving our world and the exhaustible and irreplaceable heritage that we have been given.

As human beings, we must act with a long-term perspective in mind, to reduce the economic and social gap, and to recognize that human and social issues are linked to environmental issues. The words economy and ecology are derived from the same Greek word *oikos* meaning "house." We must strive to work together to care for our common home. When we work with the earth, we can create economies of abundance and preserve our world for future generations.

PART TWO

CHAPTER 4

Nature Breaks through Prison Walls

When I was seventeen, I decided that I wanted to leave my small suburban hometown and pursue my undergraduate studies in a big city: Boston, New York, Montreal, or DC. I ended up in Quebec, only six and a half hours from where I grew up, but worlds away. I have lived in one city after the other for the last fifteen years (almost half my life): Montreal, Guayaquil, DC, Rome, and then DC again. Only now am I beginning to take seriously the call from nature to return to my roots, return to our common roots, to connect with Earth. Of course, in each place that I lived, I tried to nurture gardens, flowers on the balcony, or even house plants in my studio apartments. There is empowerment from the physical and psychological benefits of contact with non-human life, even in small doses. We do not need to live on a farm to be able to experience the beneficial effects of nature.

INCARCERATION

The United States is the world's leader in incarceration.

How did this happen?

Due to changes in law and policy, there has been a dramatic increase in incarceration rates over the last century. In 1925, the rate per 100,000 persons was 73 in state prisons and 6 in federal prisons (Bureau of Justice Statistics 1925). No data was available for local jails in 1925; however, the 1950 rate for local jails was 57 persons per 100,000. By 2016, the rate per 100,000 persons was 397 in state prisons, 53 in federal prisons, and 229 in local jails (Bureau of Justice Statistics 2016).

From 1925 to 2016, there was a 444 percent increase in the number of those incarcerated in state prisons, and a 783 percent increase in the number of those incarcerated in federal prisons. From 1950 to 2016, there was a 302 percent increase in the number of those incarcerated in local jails (Bureau of Justice Statistics 2016).

The war on drugs resulted in many people being imprisoned for drug offenses. Harsher sentencing laws (including mandatory minimums and life sentences) and less frequent parole releases have also seen people serving longer prison terms.

Where do we go from here?

That is a good question and one that has many answers: increasing treatment and prevention options, investing in long-term safety solutions, and investing in communities who have suffered disproportionately from policing policies or have been negatively affected by racial bias and socioeconomic inequality.

What does this have to do with beekeeping?

Prison education programs have positive benefits, including a lower recidivism rate, less violence, as well as increased psychological and emotional well-being. For individuals post-release, becoming a trained beekeeper can lead to increased rates of employment, learning transferrable social and workplace-related skills, and reduced rates of homelessness.

Honey bees can be a bridge between the incarcerated individual and the world outside of confinement.

SUSTAINABILITY IN PRISONS PROJECT

It was an early morning in January when I spoke with two members of the Sustainability in Prisons Project (SPP) team. Kelli Bush is the co-director and Shohei Morita is the Green Track Programs (Beekeeping and Roots of Success) coordinator. I was both in awe and humbled by their work and openness during our conversation. The Sustainability in Prisons Project is a partnership between The Evergreen State College and the Washington State Department of Corrections that provides environmental education programs in all twelve Washington state prisons. In Washington state, the incarceration rate is 256 per 100,000 people (The United States Department of Justice 2018). In total, the prison population across the state is around 19,500 people (The United States Department of Justice 2018).

I met with Kelli and Shohei over Zoom. As they sipped their morning coffee and I drank my afternoon tea, we opened by talking about the Roots of Success Program and the Beekeeping Program. Roots of Success is an environmental literacy curriculum that is peer-led, which Shohei indicated was a new model: incarcerated instructors are teaching incarcerated students. He commented that it is one of his favorite models of education, peer-based education, because it is empowering for the incarcerated participants. He also shared that they have a new gardening curriculum that is being rolled out and is also peer-led.

Sustainability in Prisons Project (SPP) is clear about what it is not: it is not a cheap source of labor, it is not designed to add stress or workload, and it is not designed to "greenwash" prisons. SPP is not trying to sustain prisons or even promote recycling, save electricity, or become Leadership in Energy & Environment Design (LEED)-certified. Their main goal is to promote sustainability through education. SPP programs were started due to the feedback of incarcerated people and corrections staff who asked for these types of initiatives. In fact, SPP has heard from formerly incarcerated partners that the programs were "lifesaving," "transformational," and/or "a valued refuge," as mentioned on their website (Sustainability in Prisons Project 2021).

All programs are voluntary. Respect for staff and participants is shown throughout the course of the program. While it is true that some SPP programs reduce operating costs and costs to taxpayers, that is not the main purpose—it is simply an added benefit. The focus is on changing lives through education, job skills, training and certification, and empowerment.

Beekeeping has been one of SPP's programs since its inception in the early 2000s. Shohei also talked about the partnership they have with the Washington State Beekeepers Association (WASBA), an organization that serves hobbyist and professional beekeepers. They help local beekeeping organizations, assist the agricultural community, and promote beekeeping and bee products. The SPP beekeeping project's primary goal is to offer formal certification education. Working with partners such as WASBA, the incarcerated beekeeping students can obtain different levels of beekeeping certifications, including apprentice and journeyman. WASBA teaches the classes and offers the hands-on aspects of beekeeping. One of the successes of the program has been that fifteen beekeepers at Airway Heights Corrections Center graduated as journeymen and authored the first draft of the journeyman manual that WASBA distributes state-wide.

Shohei is working with WASBA to develop a new craftsman-level certification for incarcerated students who are unable to earn the master-level certification due to the restrictions of the prison environment. The new certification would be available to both incarcerated individuals and anyone else who is interested. It is exciting and impressive that SPP and WASBA have been able to creatively problem-solve and propose a new level of certification that previously did not exist.

The craftsman-level certification will allow incarcerated students to keep progressing in their beekeeping knowledge and skills without the burden of fulfilling the requirements external to the prison. The craftsman-level certification will also lead to more research projects. Opportunities for research inside prisons are extremely limited, and this is an avenue through which incarcerated students will contribute to science and achieve the craftsman-level certification. The credits earned through the craftsman-level certification can also be transferred to a master-level certification upon the incarcerated student's release; this flexibility would allow some students to achieve further certification.

Staff members are another component of the success of the programs. Shohei mentioned that in prisons, there can be a sense of "us versus them" between the incarcerated people and staff. SPP is not an ideal utopia, but since the Department of Corrections staff are a vital part of the program, the collaborative nature of the project helps to mitigate some of those tensions. Everyone is learning to work with each other. Shohei said, "It's kind of cliché, but you watch the bees work together, and watching them work together is really beneficial to how the students and partners collaborate."

As of this writing, the COVID-19 pandemic has been a challenging time, especially as inmates became sick and some passed away from the virus. During the pandemic, incarcerated people have been five times more likely than the general public to become infected with the virus (University of California San Francisco 2020). By June 8, 2021, at least 398,623 people in prisons in the United States tested positive for coronavirus. As of June 8, 2021, at least 2,702 prisoners in the United States passed away from coronavirus-related causes (The Marshall Project 2021). SPP's top priority was making sure that people were safe. Most of the programs were put on hold during the pandemic, but some aspects of programming continued. SPP sent monthly packets with beekeeping articles for people to work on even in the absence of in-person meetings. They also shared documentaries through socially distanced film screenings. Even the WASBA annual conference was held remotely in 2021, which allowed a few prisons to participate remotely for the first time.

Shohei was quick to point out that there are benefits to those individuals who will remain in prison for the long term. Education promotes personal growth. Beekeeping is therapeutic in and of itself, regardless of certifications. The programs offered by the SPP do not just have educational benefits but are often stress-relieving, community-building, and hope-nurturing. It provides an opportunity for the incarcerated individuals to see themselves in a different light through positive interactions with nature.

In researching for this book, I came across many programs that focused on post-release endeavors. For people that do not have the option for release, how can beekeeping or environmental programs create a positive experience? There are many challenges that people face when returning to their communities. However, if they are not returning, are there ways to be more intentional and creative about the programs that are offered?

Kelli was clear that these programs will not make a difference for everybody. However, if someone is concerned about public safety, Kelli and SPP can appeal to them by pointing to the data around the impact of education and how it reduces recidivism. A 2005 Institute for Higher Education Policy report concluded that recidivism rates for incarcerated people who had participated in prison education programs were on average 46 percent lower than the rates of incarcerated people who had not participated in such programs (Erisman and Contardo 2005). A 2016 Rand Corporation report confirmed that individuals who participated in any type of educational program while in prison were 43 percent less likely to return to prison (Davis et al. 2014). The benefits reach beyond reducing the recidivism rate. Prisons with educational programs have less violence among incarcerated individuals. There can even be improved health outcomes.

Why should we pay for education for incarcerated people?

Kelli mentioned that there is a return on investment. In Washington state, for every dollar spent, there is a twenty-dollar return on investment. There is a possibility to reduce prison operating costs and taxpayer dollars spent. SPP has reduced costs by approximately $4.3 million each year through sustainable building operations.

When Kelli mentioned what drives her, I immediately resonated with what she said, "My heart is driven by the impacts that working with nature has on well-being and the soul." Yes. This is one of the key reasons why I wanted to write this book: to share the transformative power of nature on humans—on our hearts, minds, and emotions. There is a grasp that the natural world has on humans that can never be fully removed. I am learning to resist that grasp less and lean into it more.

Even if this program can positively affect one person, Shohei said it is worth it. Prison is not a magical utopia. It should not be. However, there are avenues to make a change and think about the world differently. The Sustainability in Prisons Project creates a ripple effect for change, especially to address social and racial inequalities—always through access to education.

SWEET BEGINNINGS

In the heart of Chicago, there is a company that has been making a buzz since 2004. Sweet Beginnings, LLC makes beelove® products, which are a natural line of raw honey and honey-infused body care products. Sweet Beginnings employs men and women returning from incarceration. In addition to developing skills in beekeeping and creating body care products, people develop confidence and find belonging in a community that invests in their personhood and success. "The best part of Sweet Beginnings is that they welcome you like a family member, they gave me a chance...They just looked at me like somebody that was coming home and part of the crew," said Johnny Patterson, honey extractor, in a You-Tube video created by the Roberts Enterprise Development Fund (Roberts Enterprise Development Fund 2017).

Sweet Beginnings, LLC was founded as part of the North Lawndale Employment Network. The company began with Brenda Palms Barber, president and chief executive officer, and her experience trying to help the unemployed access employment opportunities, in particular for people of color. "Sweet Beginnings" is a reference to a conversation Barber had with a friend about the project who commented "what a sweet beginning for them." Up until 1968, North Lawndale was a thriving community, so much so that it was economically independent from Chicago. The Civil Rights Movement and the unrest that bubbled up around it left the community struggling.

The disparity in income and quality of life between Black residents and White residents in North Lawndale was striking. Barber explains in episode two of the *Inside Sweet Beginnings* podcast, "North Lawndale was once a community where there were 125,000 residents and today, we're roughly at about 35,000. You can see the flight that took place" (Barber 2020). The community in North Lawndale had been involved in conversations about their greatest needs, with housing and employment being the top two priorities. Barber arrived in February of 1999 in the middle of their workforce development efforts in four industries: construction, manufacturing, healthcare, and childcare. She focused on developing partnerships for the first three years of the organization, while continuing to meet with the community and reassess their progress and needs.

Barber began to see a pattern in the community. There was a large population of people returning from incarceration. Although there has been a lot of progress and change over the past twenty years, at the time there was an even more burdensome stigma attached to incarceration than exists today. Barber worked for two years on a study to understand the impact of mass incarceration on the North Lawndale community. The results were astounding. Fifty-seven percent of the adults in North Lawndale had been through the criminal justice system. Barber concluded that the workforce development efforts needed to include the formerly imprisoned population to make a significant change in the community. Formerly incarcerated people are almost ten times more likely to be homeless than the general public and to be unemployed at a rate of 27 percent (higher than the total US unemployment rate during any historical period, including the Great Depression) (Couloute 2018; Couloute and Kopf 2018).

Barber then launched the U-Turn Permitted program, which is still an active four-week job readiness program offered by the North Lawndale Employment Network. However, she soon saw that the demand for the program exceeded the jobs that she was able to provide, with employers still being hesitant to hire people with criminal records. Participants had gone through job readiness training, but there was still a lack of jobs.

Barber started to think about long-term sustainability and innovative approaches to earning income. She brainstormed with her board and continued to parse out what their competitive advantage was in the marketplace and what was unique to their community in North Lawndale. Beekeeping was a last-ditch solution that came at the very end of many sessions of creative thinking. She was ready to tap out and move on; however, one of Barber's board members, Donna Ducharme, suggested beekeeping and they decided to meet up with a few beekeepers to learn more.

One of the fascinating parts of beekeeping, as Barber found out, is that there is an element of storytelling to the hobby and trade. Beekeepers learn from other beekeepers, teaching them by word-of-mouth and by actively handling the hives. You cannot learn everything you need to learn by reading a book. You need to observe the hive, interact with the bees, and get your hands dirty. You do not need a college degree or even basic literacy skills to keep bees. "I thought, wow, if that's what it requires, I think most anyone, no matter their education, no matter their work experience, could learn the art and science of beekeeping," Barber commented in a YouTube video produced by Roberts Enterprise Development Fund (Roberts Enterprise Development Fund 2017). No matter your background, anyone can learn beekeeping through working with other beekeepers. Through seed funding from the Illinois Department of Corrections and the city of Chicago, they were able to buy bees and establish the first apiary in the spring of 2004.

Working at Sweet Beginnings helps to establish an employment history for those who have been incarcerated. The unemployment rate in North Lawndale is three to five times higher than that of the city of Chicago. Nearly a quarter of the community is not working. "Having a job is more than just a revenue generator. I mean it's fundamental, but it also connects to how one sees oneself. Am I a contribution to society? It has an effect on your self-worth," Barber explains in episode two of the *Inside Sweet Beginnings* podcast (Barber 2020). It is a place that teaches them discipline and work ethic, and how to work with other people and develop positive relationships with co-workers and clients.

The recidivism rate is very low for employees of Sweet Beginnings: nationwide, 55 percent of inmates return to prison compared to less than four percent of those working at Sweet Beginnings (North Lawndale Employment Network 2008).

One of the program participants, Vonkisha Adams, demo coordinator, shared in the Roberts Enterprise Development Fund story, "I don't have any more bad in me. All I have is good. My thinking has changed. My heart has changed along with it" (Roberts Enterprise Development Fund 2017).

Sweet Beginnings began selling local honey at farmers markets and was surprised at how positive the reactions were about the quality of the honey. However, due to the low-profit margins of selling honey, Barber realized they needed to modify their product offerings. Sweet Beginnings decided to invest their time and effort into producing skincare products (lotion, body cream, lip balm) using honey and beeswax. Now, their products can be found online and in retail stores like Whole Foods and Mariano's.

There are many lessons to be learned from the bees: unity, patience, and willingness to work together. The journey of those participating in the Sweet Beginnings program mirrors that of the bees. They must learn to collaborate and to work toward the collective good. Working in nature encourages you to move at a different pace. The program encourages its participants in the exploration of their sense of self, providing a safe and supportive environment to learn and grow. As Barber thoughtfully reflected, "Something that we've learned about bees is that they don't discern between a weed or a flower. They are only interested in collecting the good and transforming that plant source into something sweet and delicious. The people that we work with, some people may see them as weeds, but we know that there is still something sweet and good that we can help transform and have a better community" (Roberts Enterprise Development Fund 2017).

CHAPTER 5

All for One, One for All

Seventeen veterans commit suicide each day in the United States (United States Department of Veterans Affairs 2020). It is an understatement to say that coming home from military service is difficult. Your life has been lived with such a high level of intensity, and the camaraderie and community are unlike any other. The strain of working on the frontlines—in wartime or peacetime—is incredibly stressful.

There are more than 18 million veterans living in the United States, according to the 2019 United States Census Bureau. Since September 11, 2001, 3.3 million veterans have served in the US military. There are around 1.4 million active-duty military service members living in the United States or deployed to more than 150 countries (United States Census Bureau 2020). Many veterans struggle to relate with others who do not understand their experiences. They may also find it difficult to reconnect with family and reestablish a role within the family, or to join or create a community.

Another challenge is finding and maintaining meaningful work and structure after having left a very ordered life in the military (United States Department of Veterans Affairs 2015). Along with the US Department of Veterans Affairs, other organizations have been founded to help veterans navigate these challenges as they readjust to day-to-day life after military service. One option that has been explored to aid veterans in their transition is beekeeping.

Beekeeping has been suggested as a vocation or hobby for veterans since the end of World War I. It was published in a pamphlet entitled "Bee Keeping. April 1919. To the disabled soldiers, sailors, and marines. To aid them in choosing a vocation." (Quick 1919). Although there is not a lot of hard data, there are plenty of stories and anecdotal evidence that have shown that beekeeping has had a positive effect on veterans, helping to lessen the symptoms of anxiety, depression, and post-traumatic stress disorder (PTSD), etc. Now, researchers are beginning to study whether beekeeping has data-driven therapeutic benefits.

Beekeeping provides veterans with a new "sense of purpose" and allows them to "block out dark thoughts" (Casey and Householder 2019). In an article in the *Military Times*, United States Army veteran Wendi Zimmerman explains, "It shows me there is a way to shut my brain down to get other things accomplished. Before, my mind would be filled with thoughts constantly and I wasn't accomplishing daily tasks" (Casey and Householder 2019). Other benefits are that beekeeping can be adapted to fit the beekeeper according to their disability or weight-lifting restrictions by procuring the proper equipment according to weight and size. It is also a quiet activity, often requiring only solo or small group work. Working with the bees encourages people to stay present in the moment. It can often be relaxing to sit and watch the bees fly in and out of the hive.

BEES4VETS

In 2017, Ginger and Daniel Fenwick started Bees4Vets, now a registered 501c3, due to the high suicide rate of veterans. They wanted to help and tried to understand what they could do in their own lives to make a difference. Daniel and Ginger both come from military families, and Ginger fell into bee-keeping through her belonging to a medieval reenactment group in which she taught a class on medieval beekeeping. Her friend offered her property to host the bees, and that is when it hit her that bees could help veterans. She had heard about a beekeeping program from West Virginia created by John McCormick. McCormick was sitting in a veterans affairs hospital waiting room and asking other people, "Hey do you want to come out to my farm and sit with the bees? It is really helping me." Ginger admired the program in West Virginia and reached out for advice on starting their program in Nevada.

During our phone call, I asked Daniel and Ginger if there was a defining moment for them in starting this program and when they knew it was worth the time and effort. Daniel said, "Four weeks in." Four weeks! Within four weeks, one of the participants had cut back his smoking dramatically, stopped drinking, and was getting off the couch. The only thing that was different in his life was attending their program. Daniel said, "If we can make that much of a change for someone in a month, at that point it was worthwhile."

Hearing from family members was also affirming for the Fenwicks. They were giving a presentation at an organization, and, unbeknownst to them, the wife of one of the participants who had completed the program was in the room. At the end of their presentation, she stood up and, in tears, informed everyone that their program had done more for her husband in one year than all the medication that the VA had tried.

Another participant was frightened of people and interacting with strangers. He could not even be in the same room as the other participants during the indoor teaching sessions. He sat in a different room in the Fenwick's home, listened, and asked questions through Ginger. There was an incredible transformation to come. For him, victory was being able to shop for groceries independently. It may not sound like a big deal. However, for him and his family, it greatly increased his quality of life and made a dramatic difference.

Daniel and Ginger are reliant on donations to support the program, which includes training, bees, and the equipment (beekeeping jackets and suits, smokers, hive tools, hive boxes), which they offer for free to participants. The program lasts about one year to learn the entire cycle of the beekeeping year. Daniel and Ginger are the main beekeeping teachers and are typically responsible for about five people each to train and supervise (approximately ten people per year in total). Along with volunteers, they make it work. They do not take a salary, and all the fundraising dollars are used to purchase the bees and equipment to support each veteran.

Ginger says that they have an open-door policy. Participants from past years are always welcome to spend time in the apiary and benefit from the camaraderie and the companionship that builds during the year-long program. Ginger says, "We're creating a family. When veterans are in the military, they have a battle buddy. They're all supporting each other. We are doing that in the apiary."

Some veterans have post-traumatic stress disorder (PTSD), a traumatic brain injury (TBI), and/or physical disabilities. Ginger is clear that while it is a beekeeping program, "We are trying to provide a place for them to learn mindfulness. How to stay in the moment." If you have 60,000 bees flying in your face, you need to stay in the moment, pay attention, and focus. Bees4Vets has partnered with a professor at the University of Nevada, Reno, who studies PTSD to research whether beekeeping is helping veterans in the Bees4Vets program.

A tradition in beekeeping that I love and have done myself is called "telling the bees." When someone experiences a death, you go "tell the bees" and share it with them. They are a listening ear. If you are angry, go "tell the bees." The bees can handle it. You can work through your emotions and verbally release your frustrations in a judgement-free space. Veteran Dick Holton in an article for *Edible Reno Tahoe* said, "Working with the bees heals my mind and really calms me down. You start to become really in tune with the state of the hive and can even tell when something is wrong based on the pitch of their buzzing." Holton continues, "I think it helps a lot in giving veterans a sense of purpose as well. A lot of these suicides are coming from a lack of sense of purpose or trauma from the past" (McArthur 2020).

While I have not personally experienced the traumas of military life, I have experienced other traumatic events in my past that I am trying to work through. For me, working with the bees has certainly helped. You need to be calm, concentrate on your breath, and focus your eyes and hands on the task. It is a therapeutic experience to work in collaboration with the bees, as gentle buzzes float by your ears.

One of the stories that I enjoyed the most from the conversation with the Fenwicks was that one of the volunteers would sing "Happy Birthday" to the honey bees that were emerging from their cells. Even after that volunteer stopped coming, the veterans still sing "Happy Birthday" to the bees being born. When you are singing "Happy Birthday" to a honey bee, you are not thinking about a traumatic event that happened five years ago. You stay in the moment. I, too, have appreciated this "staying in the moment" that beekeeping seems to cultivate as you continue to work with the bees over time.

In our conversation, we also touched on the beekeeping community. In my experience, the beekeeping community has been an extremely positive force. In Reno, the local beekeeping club has been very supportive of the Fenwicks. At this point in our conversation, I had to laugh because Ginger said, "We're kind of weird. We hang out with bugs. It is not fuzzy kittens or baby goat therapy." Unless they are allergic, she says that most people are willing to put on a beekeeping jacket and try it to "mark it off their bucket list." Ginger said, "Bees, much like horses or baby goats, really meet people wherever they are and whatever they need. If someone needs a big horse to walk beside them to help with PTSD, wonderful. If you want a hive in your backyard that could help you out, then try our program."

When I asked about any fears surrounding the future of bees and beekeeping, Daniel spoke up and mentioned that the average age of a beekeeper in the United States is over 60 years old. As people age, we will need to replenish the beekeeping community with younger beekeepers. Speaking at schools is an option to spread the word and involve children early in their lives—to encourage children to think about the environment and the role of bees in our world, and to take positive action in small ways.

As I closed my time with the Fenwicks, I was in awe of their persistence to continue their program and their commitment to veterans. Ginger shared with me what one of the veterans said to her, "I don't know what it is about these bees. I just love them." I loved Ginger's reply, "Well, it is because they have more arms to hug you with." At the end of our call, I was so moved. It was an honor to hear the stories of these veterans and to share more about this program with the world. I hope that beekeepers near and far will consider inviting a veteran to their apiary or beekeeping program. Once veterans leave the military, they lose the whole team that they were a part of, so if we can have a welcoming place or community for them to belong to, why not invite them? It just might change their life.

MISSION BEELIEVE

Monica Schmitt began beekeeping due to her son, Tristan Bannon, and his interest in keeping bees. They signed up to take a beginning beekeeping class at Carroll Community College together. And, as they say, the rest is history. Being with the bees was a great distraction from life's problems. Tristan moved to Oregon for a few years to work on an organic farm but returned to the East Coast to help Monica found Mission Beelieve.

In the years before the establishment of the organization, Monica had been building the apiary, attending conferences, and learning from other beekeeping organizations. When she first joined Carroll County Beekeepers Association, she felt that there was a friendly competition with other local beekeeping associations. She started going around the state and learning about other local clubs as well as attending the national conferences. She felt there were a lot of different organizations that were doing the same thing, but many of them were not working closely together. She wanted to change that and create more connections. Monica worked to unify beekeeping organizations and support each other.

She mentioned Sarah Red-Laird, founder of the Bee Girl Organization, and how they met at the American Beekeeping Federation conference in 2019. All the connections that Monica was able to make across the country speaks to the acceptance and willingness to share life with each other. As Monica said, "The beekeeping community doesn't see you by race. They don't care about politics or religion. They don't discriminate. If you walk funny or dress crazy, it doesn't matter. They just want to talk bees and they respect you as a beekeeper."

In 2019, she was working with a veteran who had cancer. Due to his illness, he started to have trouble taking care of his bees. Monica shared her dream about starting a bee-keeping organization, and he pushed her to accomplish her goals and helped her make connections to launch the non-profit. Unfortunately, he passed away in February of 2020. Monica took that as a sign that she could not let him down and that she had to move forward to found the organization. Monica and Tristan officially launched Mission Beelieve in 2020.

Monica shared the story about a veteran firefighter she had been working with over the last three years. She stated, "He's told me many times that if it wasn't for beekeeping, he doesn't think he'd still be with us." She uses those words as encouragement to continue helping others. She explained that they keep bees and help with pollination, but it really is about the internal change of each person. Monica continued, "It's very therapeutic, and really helps you stay on task. You work through things in life and realize that sometimes we make things harder than they really have to be."

As Monica told more of the story about her firefighter participant, she mentioned that having a purpose was important. When she first met him, he did not talk to anyone at the meetings, and he sat in the back. "A lot of people that are suffering from PTSD are loners and they feel like they do not have a purpose, that they don't belong anywhere," she explained. Now, he talks to everyone in the club, and he attends events with them. He has his own woodworking business and builds hive equipment. "He was not capable of doing any of that before beekeeping," Monica shared. One of the goals of the organization is to teach veterans how to build one-on-one relationships and to understand that everyone is on common ground with each other. When I asked Monica what we can learn from honey bees, she said, "They are a great example of an all-for-one mentality."

Monica works hard on the vocational aspect of the program, focusing on building equipment, selling bees and products from the hive, and rearing queens. This enables veterans to create a second revenue stream while also working with the bees and helping themselves mentally and therapeutically.

She believes strongly in education. Mentor support and connection to a community are very important but having advanced education in combination with these other factors will lead to success. There are many facets of the program that will help people. As she shared, "There's nothing more gratifying to hear someone say that 'you saved my life.' It makes everything that I've done—all the crying and almost giving up—worthwhile." They do not have to lose someone. The family will not have to go through the trauma of losing their loved one. Monica emphasized, "If they are healing and able to learn to deal with their PTSD in a positive manner, it affects not just the individual, but it affects their families and their relationships—it is a chain reaction." The building-up of community is truly a remedy for healing after military service.

HIVES FOR HEROES

I also had the opportunity to connect with another inspiring organization, Hives for Heroes. Steve Jimenez, founder and United States Marine Corps veteran, was very effusive and personable on our Zoom call. On the *Veteran Founder Podcast*, Steve explained that when he was transitioning back from the military, he threw himself into work as a coping mechanism thinking financial responsibility was the most important aspect of life. He realized he needed to readjust after the dissolution of his marriage and in conversations he had with his children (Carter 2020). He also struggled with alcohol and explained, "My depression was so bad sometimes that I would drink all day" (Carter 2020). He notes that his life is different now, almost two and a half years sober.

Hives for Heroes started with one of Steve's friends who wanted to keep bees. Steve said that they began with about twelve veterans in 2018. Soon after beginning, people from across the country were contacting Hives for Heroes to become involved and to ask if there were any programs in their local area. Along with Morgan Hill, who works on all aspects of marketing, they formed a team to spread the word about beekeeping as an option for "heroes," which Steve emphasized is not exclusive to veterans. Their mission is connection through purpose (beekeeping and conservation) and relationships (1:1 mentorship).

The concept is simple and only a few elements are needed: a hive, a beekeeper, and a NewBEE (participant). Hives for Heroes teaches the NewBEEs how to become entrepreneurs by matching them with a mentor and providing the hands-on experience necessary to build their own businesses. Mentors are not required to be veterans. As the program grew, there was a need to create roles for regional leaders. Now, only a few years after having founded the organization, they have almost 4,000 participants in all 50 states and have expanded to Australia. They are creating revenue streams through apiary management and merchandise sales on their website that funnels back into the program and fuels additional veteran-mentor relationships.

For Steve, beekeeping reminded him of a pseudo-combat experience: suiting up, having your tools, and preparing for a mission. "You learn how to breathe and work through the stress. You can calm yourself and control your physiology at a certain point," Steve explained.

We talked for nearly an hour about the ups and downs of beekeeping, including the loss of his first hive. Steve's experience matched my own—we were both in tears at having lost the bees, knowing that we had been responsible for taking care of them. Steve shared, "It was under my charge. My thought process was, 'I can't even do that.' These creatures have been around thousands of years, but they die from my failure." The reason Hives for Heroes offers a peer-to-peer mentoring program is that individually we often quit. Steve continued, "When we are alone and we're isolated and we feel like we can't do something, we quit." When he lost his first hive, Steve called his mentor Steve Dunn who told him, "It's okay. This is your first time doing this, and you're starting from the most difficult situation." This support provided Steve with the confidence to move forward and to help other people in the same situation.

When I asked Steve what we can learn from the bees, he answered, "Almost everything." The correlation with the military is easy to understand. Both entities have a goal and a mission larger than one's own individual interest. Bees, like military personnel, work together to achieve their outcomes. Each member of the military understands their role. It is the same with the bees. All for one, one for all.

Steve also talked about the importance of beekeeping as a family activity. It enriches relationships and allows people to spend time together doing something positive and productive. Morgan said, "You learn how to care for something. They are checking on something else. You do have to slow down and be more intentional." Some of the people that are participating in the program were not very engaged with their families due to their own trauma and experiences of post-military life.

Now, beekeeping is a family activity. There are kids in the program who are interested in beekeeping because of a parent or caregiver that is a participant. As Steve explained on the *Veteran Founder Podcast*, "When you put purpose in somebody's life and they find that purpose, which we consider a lifelong hobby of beekeeping, and you build relationships in their local communities, they become stronger." (Carter 2020).

Steve continued, "We have a question that we ask of our veterans and mentors when they come in, 'What brings you joy? If you could do anything for the rest of your life, what would you do?' We don't want people to burn out. Many hands make light work. We want people to be empowered in doing things that we want to do but not have to be chained to it. When that happens, you see their personality come out. The creativity comes out" (Carter 2020).

Steve has been honored as *Houston Business Journal*'s 40 under 40 and received the Texas Business Hall of Fame Future Texas Legend Award. He is also pursuing an MBA at Rice University in Houston, Texas, while maintaining a wonderful relationship with his daughters. Hives for Heroes is working to create a self-sustaining model by 2023, tirelessly working to develop partnerships. They have a goal of employing veterans full-time in leadership positions in communities across the country to "save bees and save vets."

HEROES TO HIVES

Heroes to Hives was founded in 2015 by United States Army veteran Adam Ingrao and his wife, Lacey. Four years after his transition from service, he was trying to find his next mission that allowed him to serve his country. When he found beekeeping, it all clicked. He started working in a bee lab during his undergraduate studies. He then moved to Michigan to begin his graduate degree in entomology. Now, Adam is an agricultural entomologist at Michigan State University (MSU) Extension. Since its inception, more than 900 military veterans and their dependents have participated in the Heroes to Hives program.

Through a free nine-month beekeeping training course, participants are encouraged to work on their own personal and financial wellness and build community and friendships with the other veterans and their families. Participants are educated in beekeeping and the importance of the pollinators' role in agriculture. In an article written for the *Military Times*, Adam stated, "'Beekeeping affords us the opportunity to really kind of engage in a different way with the natural world. You're not thinking about what happened in Afghanistan or Iraq. You're thinking about what's happening right here, right now'" (Casey and Householder 2019).

In my conversation with Adam over Zoom, he discussed how the program started with just he and his wife running the program at their farm. They were funding the entire program themselves to support five veterans. When they moved to MSU, Adam had a conversation with Dr. Meghan Milbrath to explore if there was interest in bringing the program to MSU. Adam realized that there were two options: either develop their own non-profit or find an organization that would allow them to operate under them. The partnership with MSU allowed them to both increase capacity and receive grant money to fund the program. Since 2018, the program has been run as part of the MSU Extension program.

Adam said that at the end of the first season, they hosted a harvest workshop to extract the honey. The wife of one of the veterans (a Navy seal with a 12-year enlistment) came up to Adam and told him that it feels as though her husband was working toward something greater. The skillset that you learn in the military transfers over to beekeeping very well: taking care of equipment, training, etc. Adam has heard repeatedly that the beekeeping course serves as a community development program. It is not just about learning to be good beekeepers, but it is about having veterans come together and feel normal. As Adam explained during our talk, "A lot of times we don't feel normal within regular society because of the things we've done and seen. And this is an opportunity to feel part of something greater."

As we discussed what we can learn from the bees, Adam highlighted the collective goal and working toward a common mission as a parallel experience to being in the military. Adam shared, "When I think about my battery or my company that I worked for in the military, it was the same thing." The military units have division of labor, just like a beehive. He continued, "My bees give me solace and the ability to slow things down for the time that I'm in the backyard." It is a practice to keep himself centered.

Heroes to Hives is now working with the Department of Veterans Affairs to run a research study on long-term, longitudinal health benefits of individuals who participate in programs like Heroes to Hives. They are working with the Manchester VA in New Hampshire, which is the first VA to have a beekeeping program as part of their recreational therapy department. Students will be wearing technology that will monitor their heart rates and stress levels before and after they go into the apiaries. They will also take a read of these levels one week after they have been in the apiary. They hope to publish the results by 2023. I, for one, cannot wait to read the study and look forward to hearing more about this project in the future.

While beekeeping is still being studied for its effects on veterans, the anecdotal evidence is certainly positive. As our society and government consider programs to support those who served our country, beekeeping should be included as an option for further exploration. The magnitude of the change that has occurred in the lives of the men and women who have participated in beekeeping programs cannot be underestimated. While beekeeping may be met with quizzical comments from those unfamiliar with the trade, the results are no joke.

CHAPTER 6

Beekeeping Across the World

Antarctica is the only continent that does not have bees. Bee-keeping can be found in countries all over the world with traditions spanning back thousands of years and is often passed down from generation to generation. It is truly amazing to think bees have accompanied humans throughout revolutions, wars, births, deaths—all while remaining resilient to the circumstances in which they found themselves.

Beekeeping has been intertwined in the livelihoods of farmers and homesteaders for centuries. Among the products produced by bees are honey, beeswax, pollen, propolis, and royal jelly. These can be transformed into candles, skincare products, and mead (an alcoholic beverage created by fermenting honey with water). Beekeeping can also contribute to both free and income-generating pollination services.

Now, beekeeping is practiced in both urban and rural areas. I have witnessed bees on rooftops in the middle of Washington, DC—flying to-and-fro, foraging on flowers planted in front of luxury hotels and on weeds in abandoned city lots—as well as in countryside meadows. The adaptability of bees as a species speaks to their ability to live and survive even in locations that were previously thought unsuitable. This is great news for the global population and the future of projects involving bees as we can manage and maintain beehives in varying climates and landscapes.

BEEKEEPING AND THE UNITED NATIONS SUSTAINABLE DEVELOPMENT GOALS

The importance of honey bees for global food security has become more widely recognized in the last two decades. Bees, whether native or non-native species, wild or managed populations, can contribute positively toward the achievement of the United Nations Sustainable Development Goals (SDG) particularly SDG2 (zero hunger) and SDG15 (life on land) (The 17 Sustainable Development Goals).

Bees could also contribute to other Sustainable Development Goals in addition to the two aforementioned goals (Patel et al. 2021), including but not limited to SDG1 (no poverty), SDG4 (quality education), SDG5 (gender equality), SDG8 (decent work and economic growth), SDG11 (sustainable cities and communities), and SDG13 (climate action).

Bees could help end hunger, achieve food security, and improve nutrition. All of this could be attained primarily through their pollination services, and also by offering alternative income sources that can contribute to economic stability and economic mobility. Economic development will allow more people to purchase nutrient-dense food items that tend to be more expensive or allow them more leisure time that could be used to prepare foods (rather than relying on unhealthy convenience foods).

Ensuring the survival of different bee species will stave off further biodiversity loss. For the ecosystem to function properly and abundantly, we need everything from microbes to mammals.

Strengthening the livelihoods of people through beekeeping relies upon several factors: natural, human, physical, social, and financial (Food and Agriculture Organization of the United Nations).

- Natural: bees, water, sunshine
- Human: skills, knowledge, health, strength
- Physical: tools, equipment, transportation, energy
- Social: help from the community, access to markets
- Financial: cash, savings, credit, grants

Without one of these assets, it is difficult to build a successful and sustainable livelihood. Technical, vocational, and tertiary education (target 4.3 of the Sustainable Development Goals) leads to employment and entrepreneurial activities (target 4.4, 8.6). Keeping bees provides both income and livelihood diversification (target 1.1, 8.2) and contributes to increased farm productivity when coupled with an existing farm enterprise (with the potential for an additional revenue stream through the sale of bee products) (target 1.4).

Programs that have been sponsored and funded by international agencies often pair beekeeping with another initiative, for example, tree planting and orchard enterprises. Tree planting and beekeeping are the perfect pair because bees thrive on highly diverse flora, and the protection of indigenous trees is a win-win for the bees and the trees. Nurturing existing trees and creating tree nurseries can help to conserve forests. The combination of bees and plants both improves pollination and increases crop yields. Pollination also helps enhance nutritional value (target 2.2) and improves the shelf life of fruits and vegetables (reducing food waste) (target 12.3).

However, it should be noted that national non-profits and regional organizations are often more successful at establishing connections with local producers due to effective communication and knowledge of the area. International organizations may import tactics that are not adaptable to the local condition, imposing their way as the best way, rather than considering the cultural, political, social, and economic environment of each place.

The success of these initiatives relies upon using indigenous bees, also known as local bee species. In this regard, it is also important to recognize that many resources are focused on European honey bees and specific climate zones. To be successful, these programs need to take into account the type of bees and the climate indicators that may vary from the Western-produced literature.

Beekeeping is very hands-on, and training must be practical, using demonstrations and real-life experiences to pass on knowledge and not just relying on theory or written content. Beekeeping is a cyclical process, and a full year cycle must be learned, under the guidance of an experienced beekeeper before the student beekeeper can work alone.

Another necessary component for successful beekeeping is reliable transportation. If beekeepers cannot travel, they may not be able to access markets to sell their products. Building and/or sourcing the proper equipment is another challenge. Equipment must be appropriate to the community. Importing foreign equipment often does not work and requires the replacement of parts that are hard to come by.

For example, frame equipment should not be used unless it can be manufactured locally. Many countries with larger manufacturing facilities rely upon this equipment, but if it cannot be created locally, it is more hassle than it is worth. Beekeepers will be unable to continue working with bees if they cannot find replacement equipment. Beekeepers also need extractors to gather the honey, containers to store the honey, taps and filters to strain the honey, and refractometers to measure the water content of honey.

Several organizations across the world are carrying out this work to introduce beekeeping in areas where there is not an established history of formalized beekeeping for economic development. I must admit that while these brief profiles are not exhaustive, they do highlight real change that is happening in the lives of people in different parts of the globe through beekeeping.

UNDER THE MANGO TREE

Agriculture supports more than half of India's population. Under The Mango Tree was founded in 2009 as a hybrid enterprise by Vijaya Pastala to improve rural incomes and diversify livelihoods. The name evokes a beautiful image of rest and connection, as farmers often sit "under the mango tree" to escape the sun in the dry, arid regions of India. As explained on their website, "Each group [from villagers to traders]—rested and more learned—moves on. Yet, each individual will remember the respite offered by the mango tree's shade" (Our Story, Under the Mango Tree).

I spoke with Sujana Krishnamoorthy, executive director of Under The Mango Tree Society, over Google Meet. She mentioned that their primary goal was to fix the issue of market access for small farmers. She explained that 86 percent of farmers in India are small and marginal holders, owning less than two hectares (or five acres) of land. The farming tends to be rain-fed, which means that most of it is subsistence agriculture (food grown for household consumption).

Access to equitable markets was a problem for farmers who were often exploited and did not have a reliable network of buyers. Compensation was also an issue as these smallholder farmers were not receiving a just price for their goods. Vijaya realized that due to India's diverse flora, there abounded a variety of regional honey that could be sold to interested buyers, especially in urban areas. There is beautiful eucalyptus honey from near the Himachal Pradesh and Punjab border, tulsi honey from the foothills of the Himalayas, wild forest honey from the Narmada River valley, and litchi (lychee) honey from the lowland region of northern India, just to name a few.

Urban consumers were delighted by the different flavors, often remarking that it reminded them of honey that they had when they were children. Farmers could add honey bees, the indigenous *Apis cerana indica* in particular, to their farms to add a commodity product to their inventory as well as receiving the cross-pollination benefits for their crops.

Under The Mango Tree invests in long-term relationships with its partners and in sustainability in all forms. They have established a fair-trade market for locally produced honey. Under The Mango Tree Society, the non-profit sister to the for-profit Under The Mango Tree Naturals and Organics Private Ltd., focuses on training smallholder farmers to use bees to increase their income by 40 percent. These farmers live below the poverty line, which is about two dollars per day by international standards. They also work on community outreach, research, and policy advocacy to advance sustainable community-based beekeeping and the well-being of the farmers and ecosystem.

As of 2019, they have expanded to 175+ villages across fourteen districts. Sujana mentioned that over the last ten years they have worked with over 70,000 farmers. The team of two that was once Vijaya and Sujana has now grown to about 80 people across three states in India.

Sujana and Vijaya met and had both been involved in the development sector in India. They worked together to create the Bees for Poverty Reduction Program, building it based on feedback and research about beekeeping courses offered by the government. The government course was held at a training institute for fifteen to twenty days, in which students would receive instruction, but they would not work directly with the bees in a farm setting. They did not learn the seasonal aspect of beekeeping or witness the rhythms of bees in real life. After returning to their farms with bees in hand, they were puzzled by bee behaviors that did not follow the textbook. In a few months, most of the bees absconded and the activity came to a dead end.

Under The Mango Tree Society recognized the need to have a practical component for the farmers to pick up on the key aspects of beekeeping throughout the seasons. They also teach in the local language. Sujana mentioned that the first two years of Under The Mango Tree Society were difficult because it required a knowledge shift for the farmers to accept beekeeping into these communities. They relied on word-of-mouth testimonies and evidence of increased yields of mangoes and cashews to convince farmers about the impact of bees on agriculture.

Under The Mango Tree Society also works with tribal communities, people who are marginalized and live close to the forest, who have traditionally practiced "honey hunting." These honey hunters explore the jungles for beehives. They then would squeeze the combs to extract honey, and, in the process, the bees would die. They also undertook other unsustainable practices, including burning the hives. Under The Mango Tree Society started working with these honey hunters to become "colony spotters" instead, in which they would transfer colonies found in the wild into boxes. This process not only allowed the bees to survive and produce more honey over time but also contributed to an awareness campaign about the importance of bees for agricultural yields.

Sujana shared with me a testimony from one of the honey hunters, who sometimes hunted seven to eight colonies per day. This honey hunter looked back at the damage he had caused to the ecosystem and now understands that other methods benefit both the bees and humans. Under The Mango Tree Society has now introduced a system where entire communities take a pledge that they will stop honey hunting and pass on the message to their relatives and friends in other villages.

Under The Mango Tree Society also works with local carpenters to make the bee boxes and women's self-help groups to make the beekeeping veils. In each village, two or three beekeepers are trained as "master trainers" with advanced beekeeping skills to help the rest of the beekeeping community through its cycles. They also started to introduce bee-friendly plants into these areas to increase forage for bees. Under The Mango Tree Society has truly created a supportive ecosystem around beekeeping.

While Under The Mango Tree Society improves the local regions through beekeeping, they also have been creating a pilot program to assist with earning additional income and increasing proper nutrition. As I asked Sujana about climate and the environment, Sujana mentioned that in the last three years, they have piloted a kitchen garden concept. In many communities, they were only growing one crop and relying on the rain. The land would lay fallow during the other months of the year outside of that crop season. The team brainstormed ways to make sure that there would be enough forage for bees from February to May.

The kitchen garden concept uses gray water (water from washing and bathing) to grow gourds, cucumbers, and other produce that grows easily and quickly. Through this program, farmers added vegetables to meet their own nutritional needs, but they were also able to sell any surplus in the local markets. This process is a very effective climate change-proof technique because these areas were dry and already prone to drought.

One of the most impactful stories that Sujana told me was that many families have stopped migrating for short-term agricultural work to earn money. Families have been able to stay in one place and have more stability due to the extra income earned from the surplus of their produce and honey sales. This means that children can stay in school and receive a formal education—an extremely powerful effect of introducing beekeeping to these communities.

The challenge is to convince the government that these beekeeping techniques are more suitable than importing hybrid European bees or focusing only on honey production. The evidence that Under The Mango Tree Society has seen over the last ten years is that their method makes sense for smallholder agriculture—to use indigenous bees, to focus on local production, and to include environmentally-friendly practices.

EARTHBEAT SOLUTIONS FOUNDATION

Gold mining is extremely dangerous and, yet it is one of the only options for income in parts of Uganda. The industry is poorly regulated, rife with corruption, lacks transparency, and allows for ongoing human rights abuses. The negative impacts affect both people (child labor, exposure to toxic chemicals, lack of safety gear, harsh conditions) as well as the environment (destroying pastureland) (Monks 2018).

Many people were dying in a mining community in Busia, Eastern Uganda. Guya Merkle, founder of the Earthbeat Solutions Foundation, talked directly with the community to understand if they were interested in other economic opportunities, and what they would like to pursue. Their answer: beekeeping. In 2016, the Earthbeat Solutions Foundation created the Heartbeat Honey Project to offer an alternative income possibility to gold miners through beekeeping (Earthbeat Solutions Foundation 2018). With the help of local experts, The Hive, Ltd., a privately-owned company, 80 gold miners and community members began training as beekeepers. The Hive teaches people both the theory and practical elements of beekeeping.

Other annual crops are susceptible to droughts and harsh weather; however, working with the environment through beekeeping was a much more promising and manageable endeavor. As a bonus, the production of crops has increased since the introduction of the bees, due to their pollination activity. As Kabuubi Abubaker Aziz, one of the trainers at The Hive, explains in the documentary *Liquid Gold*, "It is a permanent source of income, a permanent source of sustainability" (Elson 2018). The opportunity for sustained income for people in rural areas, regardless of social and economic status, is real and possible (Sustainable Development Goals, targets 10.1 and 10.2). The impact is slow as the hives and colonies need to mature before being ready to harvest honey. However, there is great hope for the future.

One of the Busitema beekeepers, Omeda Samuel, explains that beekeeping provides a solution that is also advantageous to the environment, unlike mining which is ravaging the landscape. "It is very important when people think of money, to first think of the environment...Once we destroy it, then we are destroying our lives" (Elson 2018).

The outcome looks promising, and it has been empowering for the participants, especially for the women. Taaka Lydia, a participant and member of the Siyanyonja Women in Mining Association, shared, "I have the dream that as a woman, I stand on my own" (Elson 2018). Beekeeping offers a space for everyone, young and old, man or woman. Beekeeping can be an avenue for the empowerment of women (SDG target 5.5), even in traditionally patriarchal societies. The industry is ripe for expansion and further inclusion.

BEES FOR DEVELOPMENT
Bees for Development, founded in 1993, focuses on building local capacity and partnering with local organizations to accomplish their work in Central and Southeast Asia, Eastern Europe, Central and South America, and Africa, particularly in Ethiopia, Ghana, and Uganda. By building capacity with local partners, they can lead development in

their own countries and communities. Bees for Development promotes self-sufficiency and ownership of the beekeeping process. They offer education and training about sustainable apiculture, as well as a journal and online library. The free journal focuses on beekeeping technologies and lessons from different countries and is available to download on their website.

They are adamant about promoting local-style, fixed-comb hive beekeeping with local bees and local materials (instead of the frame hive systems that I have mentioned previously) due to accessibility, cost, and respect for location. If the input cost is low, the barrier to entry will be low. For example, in Ghana, they teach people to hollow out the *Borassus* palm which makes a wonderful nest for the bees. The green palm fronds can be used to weave cylindrical hives and palm fiber can be used for smoker fuel (Bees for Development Journal April 2021).

As proponents of natural beekeeping, they support the bees' natural behavior and the genetic fitness of the population. With this method, beekeepers will follow the rhythms and signs from the bees and the world around them to dictate their choices and decisions in managing the hives.

In working with beekeepers directly, Bees for Development helps them to access fair and reliable markets for their produce. In turn, this increases incomes for poor families to meet their basic needs, while also benefiting the environment through pollination services, biodiversity conservation, habitat restoration, and economic incentives for forest maintenance (Our Story, Bees for Development). Even during the COVID-19 pandemic, beekeeping has proven to be more resilient than other industries; beekeeping has continued outdoors, and honey prices are rising, both of which bode well for beekeepers.

While beekeeping is not a new industry in Ethiopia, Bees for Development has partnered with local leaders and community members to identify families and individuals most in need to participate in their program. One of these participants, Mulat Abie from Ethiopia, trained to become a beekeeper during the COVID-19 pandemic. Abie, who has suffered from a mental disability most of his life, said, "I feel proud and confident, and I see other people's attitudes have changed toward me" (Bees for Development May 2021).

Beekeeping has offered an option for landless people. In Ethiopia, for example, agricultural land is becoming scarce as the vast majority of arable land has been allocated to families through a certification process that took place in the 1990s and 2000s (Bees for Development January 2021). Landless young people are more likely to experience food insecurity due to their lack of land and the reality that they must spend a large portion of their budget on food.

Luckily, bees do not need a large space to nest in and can be hosted on very small plots of land. Worknesh Abe is a young woman who needed to find an income source beyond farming due to her lack of land ownership. She has been trained through Bees for Development and is now able to send her children to school. She said, "If we did not have bees, I would have sent my son to work as a shepherd, not to school" (Bees for Development January 2021). This is leading to more economic resiliency and viability for the landless population, as well as educational advancement for their children.

The work of beekeeping is interdependent with that of plants and the greater ecological system. Plants provide nectar to bees and bees pollinate the plants for reproduction. It is possible to undertake beekeeping in a way that is sustainable and beneficial to humans, animals, plants, and the environment as a whole. As humans, we need to be conscious about our actions to preserve nature and reduce the negative behaviors that impact our ecosystem. Beekeepers will be the first to tell you that we need to conserve and promote floral diversity— without it, the bees do not live well, and humans will also face long-term consequences.

Efforts to expand beekeeping are underway in countries across the world, in developed and developing nations. I know from my own experience living in various climates (freezing cold Montreal and stifling hot Guayaquil), we need to adapt to the rhythms of the animals themselves. Bees will teach us the times and patterns that work best to care for them. We just need to be observant and willing to adjust. Resources from governments and non-governmental sources will be crucial to continue beekeeping programs, especially in places that do not have an established beekeeping community. I have great hope for a brighter future, where honey bees and humans live in harmony, helping each other to move forward in alignment with our deepest values and creating a bountiful world in which everyone flourishes.

PART THREE

CHAPTER 7

Revitalization, Conservation and Education

You cannot escape Mother Nature.

Whether in a city or the country, the breeze blows freely. You cannot tame it.

The ability to connect with nature, in the middle of a city, is invaluable. Even the smallest interaction with nature can help change people's minds and mentalities, and even benefit their health and well-being. After living in an urban environment for the past fifteen years, I know how vital the sound of birds, the feel of fresh air, and a day without sirens are for my sense of peace. I am still learning to balance these conflicting parts of myself: the city-loving part that enjoys the access to museums and concerts and the country-loving part that wants to plant her feet in the soil and rub arms with the meadows instead of strangers on the Metro.

Working with bees—these incredible creatures—is fascinating and a little unnerving at first. One of the most fulfilling parts of beekeeping is being a part of the community of people that care about bees, whether that includes beekeepers themselves and/or people that are supporting bees and other pollinators. Most often the beekeepers that I meet are very involved in their local communities. Their efforts are not focused solely on selling honey, but, rather, they often offer educational activities to help schools or communities to learn more about bees.

DETROIT HIVES

In the heart of Detroit, Timothy Paule and Nicole Lindsey are transforming vacant lots into urban bee farms and pollinator habitats to create sustainable communities. Detroit is one of those cities that has endured dark and difficult times. Detroit's motto is *Speramus meliora; resurget cineribus*, which means "We hope for better things; it shall arise from the ashes" (Encyclopedia of Detroit). The motto is attributed to Fr. Gabriel Richard after a terrible fire destroyed most of Detroit on June 11, 1805. The city was leveled by the fire, but the people were hopeful that they could rebuild.

Since 1950, Detroit has lost 60 percent of its population to urban flight (Angelova 2012). On June 18, 2013, the City of Detroit filed for bankruptcy, the nation's largest municipal bankruptcy. There was a mass exodus away from the city, but many remained and refused to give up. A year later, on December 10, 2014, the City of Detroit exited bankruptcy.

In 2016, Detroit launched a citywide endeavor to repurpose abandoned lots to revitalize the community. Paule and Lindsey, both Detroit natives, conceptualized some unique solutions for the community: a peacock farm, an urban campsite, an outdoor photography studio, and a community garden. The origin of Detroit Hives started in 2016 after Paule personally experienced the benefits of local raw honey from a Ferndale store owner. The raw honey contributed to curing a cold after he had tried other unsuccessful treatments. His grandmother had always created home remedies, and he decided to return to those methods to treat his ailments.

The more they learned about honey bees and the medicinal properties of honey, the more the idea for urban honey bee farms solidified into something plausible. They enrolled in local beekeeping classes at Green Toe Gardens and with the "Sweet on Detroit" program.

Paule and Lindsey are playing a role in the revitalization of the city and the resurgence of backyard beekeeping. They believe a healthy future for bees reflects a healthy future for humanity. As stated on their Instagram page, "The health of those in our inner-cities, specifically people of color, is often the last to be considered—it is our mission to change this" (Detroit Hives Instagram).

The two bought their first lot on the East Side of Detroit in 2017 under a community partnership with Detroit Land Bank. They launched Detroit Hives with the tri-fold mission of revitalization, conservation, and education. They were awarded a grant from Detroit SOUP, a Shark Tank-like dinner, where local entrepreneurs present proposals.

As Lindsey said in a documentary produced by Spruce Tone Films and aired by *National Geographic* in their Short Film Showcase, "Detroit is a place of innovators, creators" (National Geographic 2019). Over the years, they have grown their business through buying other lots and multiplying the number of hives.

REVITALIZATION

Detroit Hives has contributed to the revitalization of inner-city communities, showing that Detroit is "the place to bee." "You don't have to have a million dollars in your bank account to start an idea. Go for it," said Lindsey in the Spruce Tone Films story. Their mission, as a small business and a non-profit, is changing the way the city has treated beekeeping. Detroit has lifted limitations and Paule and Lindsey have inspired other residents to start their own colonies. By saying "yes" to each opportunity presented to them, Detroit Hives has grown from one lot to nine lots in the last few years.

Their revitalization efforts impact the lives of people in Detroit by cleaning up neighborhoods and adding value to the communities. The honey bees help increase the produce yield for neighborhood residents growing food in their gardens. The abandoned lots often serve as dumping grounds and can be an environmental hazard or simply an eye sore. Detroit Hives hopes to lift the stigma and transform urban blight into thriving areas where people can gather, and nature can thrive. Local artists have also contributed their talents to create murals of bee-themed artwork at their sites. Their latest idea is a motor-themed pollinator garden to honor the Motor City's history.

In 2019, there were 90,000 vacant lots in Detroit (National Geographic 2019). Since 2017, Detroit Hives has converted nine vacant lots into apiaries, maintaining 35 hives. Their efforts have led Paule and Lindsey to become full-time employees of Detroit Hives, funded through scholarships, grants, crowdfunding, donations, and tours with Airbnb Experiences (they currently hold the number one spot in Detroit). They also sell honey online, at farmers markets, on tours, and to local restaurants. Some local vendors have even created specialty products using Detroit Hives' honey such as beer (Black Bottom Brewery) and barbeque sauce (Slows Bar Bq).

CONSERVATION

Their conservation efforts provide habitats for honey bee colonies as well as native bee species. Some rural farms are plagued by chemicals. While vacant lots are simply that— untouched. The abandoned lots often are free from pesticides and herbicides due to their lack of use, which proves beneficial for the bees and helps to support bee diversity. Plants that we consider weeds, like dandelions, can often be one of the bees' favorite places to land and forage. The cross-pollination efforts of the bees allow for food to be grown to feed the local communities. Their sites also have garden plots planted with peppers, tomatoes, zucchini, squash, basil, and lavender.

EDUCATION

Detroit Hives has educated more than 2,000 students and hosted more than 500 public tours for city residents and visitors. Their educational efforts spread awareness about the importance of pollinators in our ecosystem. They are introducing beekeeping in classrooms and in other educational settings, to teach children and show them something different. "You never know where it may take them," Paule says. They are also combating fears that many residents have about bees and busting myths about their behavior, as well as misidentification with hornets and wasps. In my own experiences with teaching children and adults about bees, through hive tours or even in casual conversation, I recognize that unlocking the truth about these animals can lead to significant shifts in both attitude and behavior.

This hands-on science leads to expanded minds and an interest in exploring the natural world, even in the middle of a city. When we bring bees into classrooms for experiential learning, the children may first be afraid. It is normal. Our society has taught us to fear bees. However, the more kids learn about them, the more they realize how gentle and cooperative the honey bees are with each other. As they become educated, they become the honey bees' best advocates by telling their parents and caregivers about their experiences. Children are so curious and open, much more so than adults, and can be "bee ambassadors" to their families. I have used books, games, the "waggle dance," and live demonstrations of the hives to unveil the unique aspects of these creatures and to quell any fears.

My favorite part is answering questions from kids: "Where is the queen?" "What does she do?" "Can we taste the honey?" "Does it hurt to be stung?" "Which flowers do they like best?" "Where do they live?" Responding to comments and conversing with other people about a topic that is not fully understood by the general public is life-giving and provides purpose. It is truly a magical experience when I see the smile of a young child that has conquered one of their fears and now sees bees as friends.

DIVERSITY

In the United States, beekeepers of color are few and far between. With Paule and Lindsey in the community, younger people can see what is possible and inspire different pathways. Paule is showing children and teens that it is "cool to give back to your environment, cool to give back to your community," as he mentioned in the Spruce Tones Film story.

By cleaning up the communities, Paule and Lindsey hoped it would inspire their neighbors to care and contribute as well. "Growing up it wasn't cool to be into science or to keep bees or be outside in nature," Paule explained, "It is important to pass this information on to our next generation so that they can create a better future for themselves" (National Geographic 2019). They continue to spread their education through in-person tours, but also on their social media sites. Detroit Hives highlights Black figures that impacted bee-keeping, including Dr. George Washington Carver, who is known mainly for his research on peanuts, but was also a beekeeper at Tuskegee University, and Dr. Charles Henry

Turner, a zoologist and entomologist, who was the first to discover how honey bees can identify certain colors, patterns, and shapes.

FUTURE EXPANSION

They are hoping to grow to 200 hives in 45 locations by 2024. Lindsey and Paule would like to establish a learning center to teach year-round and are working toward Detroit becoming a Bee City. In February 2021, Detroit Hives announced that it would be opening its first location outside of Detroit in Kansas City. With their motto of "work hard, stay bumble," Detroit Hives has contributed to the resilience and revitalization of the city it calls home. Now, it will look to transform not only Detroit but also Kansas City, lot by lot, with persistence and a healthy dose of humility.

CHAPTER 8

The Buzz in the City

What do oaks, magnolias, and clover have in common? They are the top three plant species found in honey from Washington, DC, according to The Best Bees Company's honey DNA sequencing project (National Geographic 2018). Honey DNA? Yes, you read that right. Think 23andme, but for honey. I was curious to learn more, so I spoke with Best Bees and delved deeper into the world of urban beekeeping.

I have had many friends, classmates, and colleagues express surprise when I tell them that I am a beekeeper in the middle of Washington, DC. Due to the diversity of plant life within a small radius, bees can collect nectar and pollen from a greater number of species in one dense area.

If you think about Washington, DC, hotels and embassies are consistently updating their flower pots and gardens to improve the look of their spaces. There are also community gardens and, of course, DC residents' balconies and yards. While unsightly for humans, even weeds in abandoned lots are appealing to the bees.

It is hard to imagine, but beekeeping was once illegal in some cities. In most cities, beekeeping has only become legal within the last ten years. In some cases, beekeeping was happening even before cities regulated it, so in those instances, creating laws around the practice helped to codify and create acceptance in those communities.

While some regulations are useful to protect residents, honey bees are not as dangerous or as harmful as many people believe. Unless a person has a severe bee venom allergy, most of the population can breathe easy knowing that honey bees have no incentive to sting. They are not aggressive by nature, nor do they want to attack you. People tend to confuse honey bees with wasps, hornets, and other flying insects, who do have the ability to sting multiple times and are more aggressive by nature. Beekeepers bear the brunt of stings, and only because we are disturbing the hives when we do an inspection. The bees are protecting the queen, their resources (pollen, honey), and the baby brood.

Since bees have such an important role to play in our environment, there are many regulations around the care and cultivation of bees. I am thankful for all the beekeepers who paved the way before me, especially in Washington, DC.

BEE CITY USA AND BEE CAMPUS USA

How did Washington, DC (the city I have called home for the better part of ten years) become a "Bee City?" Bee City USA and Bee Campus USA are initiatives of The Xerces Society for Invertebrate Conservation. Established in 1971, the Xerces Society is a leader of invertebrate protection and uses advocacy, education, and applied research to advance conservation. Bee City and Bee Campus are now housed under the Xerces Society umbrella. There are now over 126 Bee City USA Affiliates and 107 Bee Campus USA Affiliates.

Bee City affiliates make commitments to conserve native pollinators through establishing a standing committee to advocate for pollinators, creating or enhancing native pollinator habitats, reducing the use of pesticides, incorporating pollinator-conscious practices into city policies and plans, and hosting pollinator awareness events (Bee City USA). Bee Campus affiliates also make the same pledge but also include offering courses or continuing education opportunities to incorporate pollinator conservation and service-learning projects to enhance pollinator habitats (Bee Campus USA).

These initiatives arose to address and reverse pollinator decline. This global pollinator decline is cause for great concern, on many levels, but particularly for environmental sustainability. As I mentioned previously in chapter three, there are many reasons for pollinator decline, and the approach to reverse its effects must address a multitude of factors (climate change, pesticides, and pests and pathogens). The Xerces Society guides communities on conservation efforts for native pollinators, including information on creating a healthy habitat for native bees, including but not limited to bumble bees, leafcutter bees, sweat bees, mason bees, longhorn bees, and mining bees. Taking steps to help these native bees will also help non-native honey bees, moths, and butterflies.

On June 20, 2014, President Barack Obama issued the Presidential Memorandum, "Creating a Federal Strategy to Promote the Health of Honey Bees and Other Pollinators" (Obama 2014). The national task force that was assembled to organize this effort identified key issues that affect pollinator health. Along with the aforementioned factors, they also identified land-use policies and practices. It is through this effort that DC worked to create a plan for its unique urban environment.

The Sustainable Urban Agriculture Apiculture Act, part of the Sustainable DC Omnibus Amendment Act of 2014 made beekeeping in the District legal. The District has no commercial agriculture or large-scale beekeeping due to its geographical size. It is mostly filled with backyard beekeepers and hives that are hosted at hotels, restaurants, and other businesses. Urban beekeeping has increased in recent years due to the increase in urban gardening and awareness of where food is grown. Now, there are over 500 hives registered in DC. Even in urban spaces, people are interested in returning to our roots, literally.

DC became a Bee City in 2016 through a campaign headed by the DC Department of Energy & Environment (DOEE) and Natasha Garcia Andersen. Information signs and literature about honey bees and native pollinators were installed at local garden centers. On Earth Day, thousands of packets of seeds were given away at Metro stations. Through these pollinator seed giveaways, native meadow creation, and educational outreach (among other efforts) DC fulfilled the requirements to become a Bee City.

DOEE and the DC Beekeepers Alliance continue to conduct outreach to District residents through training, presentations, and partnerships in the local community. In fact, the beginning beekeeping course offered by the DCBA was how I learned beekeeping. Agriculture and the agrarian sciences have been sought out in the last few years, and the beginning beekeeping class held by the DC Beekeepers Alliance is sold out every year with a waiting list.

GEORGETOWN UNIVERSITY BEE CAMPUS

In the summer of 2019, I put on my bee suit and met with the honey bee caretakers on Georgetown's campus, mentor and professor Dr. William Hahn, and the students of Hoya Hives. The students care for the bees by feeding them, treating for pest management, and checking the pattern of the comb to make sure the hive is healthy, and the queen is laying well.

During our conversation, Professor Hahn mentioned that we assume that nature, its products, and its processes will always be around to serve us. We often take for granted what nature provides us and overlook how precious its resources are to our well-being. Without pollinators, we would not be able to grow the diversity and quantity of plants in our region. Pollinator health is also an important measure of overall environmental quality.

Washington, DC was already a "Bee City" before Georgetown University decided to pursue the "Bee Campus" designation. It seemed like a natural next step to continue the good work of the DOEE and DC Beekeepers Alliance by moving forward with pursuing the designation for the urban campus.

Georgetown University was awarded the designation in 2020 becoming the first university campus in Washington, DC to hold this distinction. In applying for this designation, our Georgetown Bee Campus committee desired to address the issue of global pollinator decline and show environmental leadership in our local area. The committee is composed of faculty, staff, students, and community experts on bees and pollinators.

Some of the steps that were taken to improve our campus in becoming a safer habitat for pollinators and meet the requirements of the Xerces Society were: planting native plants, creating pollinator nesting sites with appropriate signage, hosting pollinator awareness events, developing new academic courses, augmenting existing courses on pollinator biology, and fostering additional learning opportunities for students.

Georgetown University has been working to develop sustainability efforts over the last few years. There is now a campus sustainability walk with signage posted with facts and interesting tidbits of information about water runoff, Leadership in Energy & Environment Design (LEED) building standards, energy efficiency, recycling, and composting. In fact, alongside the submission for Bee Campus Status, the committee was also working on applying for a grant from the university under the Laudato Si' initiative. The Laudato Si' fund is named after Pope Francis' 2015 encyclical on environmental justice. The fund supports sustainability projects that help to "care for our common home" by creating a healthier, more biodiverse ecosystem. The Bee Campus committee was awarded a grant for their project for the 2019-2020 academic year.

The goals of the Bee Campus committee that aligned with the Laudato Si' initiative were promoting cross-disciplinary research, contributing to local policy and practice dialogue about pollinator protection, educating the broader public about pollinator sustainability issues (including an event during Pollinator Week in June), preparing students as future environmental leaders, helping restore native pollinator habitats on campus and in the broader DC area, engaging in partnerships with local communities and jurisdictions, and convening leaders to discuss common problems and solutions to pollinator decline.

For National Pollinator Week 2020, the Georgetown Bee Campus team and Hoya Hive students partnered with the DC Beekeepers Alliance and the DC Department of Energy and Environment to build awareness through an initiative called the DC Pollinator Porch Parade. Residents created artwork (drawings, murals, sculptures) and signs with fun facts about birds, bees, beetles, butterflies, etc. that were featured in their yards and windows, and on porches and sidewalks. Using a parade map, people were encouraged to take walks around DC neighborhoods to learn about these fascinating creatures.

The Bee City and Bee Campus initiatives highlight the inter-connectedness of our world. We need pollinators because they contribute to overall environmental health and biodi-versity and play a major role in our food system. Human actions affect the environment, and this initiative will help to address some of these issues, including water runoff and the use of pesticides. Even understanding where honey comes from and being more involved in the local food scene can help educate consumers and instill support for local food production.

THE BEST BEES COMPANY

One company has sought to bring bees to the urban core of cities across the United States. The Best Bees Company installs and maintains honey bee hives on commercial and residential properties in urban areas across the United States. Their mission is not only to turn a profit but to improve bee health and expand the bee population. The company was founded in 2010 and is making a real impact on the state of bees in our country. The company has grown from a small local business to a nationwide endeavor. Their commitment to pollinator health works in conjunction with providing innovative solutions for businesses looking to improve their eco-footprint.

Best Bees works with businesses to put beehives on their roof-tops and in unused spaces in a win-win model, which benefits both the environment and the businesses' sustainability mis-sions. The clients know that they are participating in some-thing good for the world, and they also receive a sweet reward in the form of honey at the end of the season. Sustainability is a growing buzzword in all industries and Best Bees is growing at the perfect time.

For example, through this process of setting up beehives, buildings can also seek Leadership in Energy & Environment Design (LEED) points for LEED certification. Pollinator habitats can earn a property up to seven credits, including credits for local food protection, social equity within the community, heat island reduction, site development (protect or restore habitat), and innovation. The credit for social equity encourages engagement with community stakeholders to address the needs of vulnerable populations. Community education efforts about pollinators and expansion into underserved areas could contribute to a more sustainable environment for all people, especially those who may have little say in a building's development.

Best Bees employs scientists and data technologists, not just beekeepers. Of course, with the increased use of technology in beekeeping, some may say they are moving further away from the traditional craft and trade of beekeeping that involves daily observations and working with the bees, hands deep in the hive.

However, the company has been able to identify the top sources of plant species present in the honey they have harvested in cities across the United States. They are using technology to determine what helps and harms the bees, and how this data can potentially influence how we protect and support all species of bees, not just honey bees. Noah-Wilson Rich, chief scientific officer at Best Bees, said, "This is one species of 200,000 species of pollinators. We can't possibly study all those pollinators, so we use bees as an indicator species. We think if we do what is good for honey bees that will also help the other pollinators too" (NowThis Earth 2020).

"NEXT GEN" BEEKEEPERS

I was fortunate to talk with Paige Mulhern, creative director at Best Bees, and share some time together over Zoom to discuss their innovative approach to beekeeping. Best Bees has created an informative and uplifting series on their website and social media pages spotlighting the next generation of beekeepers. This series was inspired by Sarah Red-Laird, founder of the Bee Girl Organization, who started the concept of "Next Gen" beekeepers. Best Bees wanted to support her and her initiative, which is focused on education and awareness about bees and pollinators, especially education for children.

The majority of beekeepers on the Best Bees team are 30 years old or younger, and it is a fresh group of people that have become involved in the beekeeping world. The idea is to shake up the idea of a beekeeper beyond the older White male. They are looking to diversify the industry and the series has contributed to that conversation. I can picture myself as a "Next Gen" beekeeper and feel at home among my peers that are highlighted in their series. Beekeeping is a worthwhile and attainable activity for all ages, young and old. It is becoming a more welcoming and inclusive activity, which is refreshing.

ART AND SCIENCE

Best Bees blends the art and science of beekeeping through using technology to supplement their beekeeping practices and using the data to contribute to research on honey bees and other pollinators. To track trends, it helps to have the technology to capture what the bees are telling them. They have a proprietary app called Buzz that was developed in-house. It serves as the central database for their hive inspections, keeping track of beekeeping routes that now number in the tens of thousands.

Their beekeeping practice is very standardized (down to the types of boxes and pest treatments they use), so everything is scalable, and the data will be very cohesive. Through this practice, they have a very reliable control group of bees who are experiencing similar interventions across the United States.

Best Bees also collaborates with the National Aeronautics and Space Administration (NASA), one of their research partners, to implement the data collected into different research projects that they are undertaking. I found this mind-blowing! My former roommate from college, Jenni Sidey-Gibbons, was selected to become an astronaut with the Canadian Space Agency in 2017, and I immediately thought of her when I heard about this initiative.

NASA is overlaying where beehives are located with climate mapping to see if there is a correlation between beekeeping and climate change. This will help to look at bee health and compare the two to see if there are conclusions that can be drawn. During our conversation, Paige mentioned that they do not have the capacity to run these year or multi-year projects themselves, but they will share their data with other partners so that they can work together as a collective.

HONEY DNA

Honey DNA is a program that started in 2017 and benefits not only honey bees but also native pollinators and solitary bees. Best Bees samples honey from their client hives and partners with a lab in Denver that performs genomic sequencing of the honey. The lab looks at the proteins in the honey and analyzes the DNA of those proteins to determine what type of pollen is in the honey.

Through this science, the lab can discover what exact species of flower or tree the bees have visited. They can better understand the diet of the bees and how that is linked to their overall health. A diversified diet is one of the bees' best defenses against predators and environmental stressors. For example, if a bee is foraging on 75 percent clover in Boston, Best Bees could use this data to suggest the purchase of a more diverse selection of plants for the city's landscaping and beautification projects.

In DC, for example, there are multiple sources that bees forage for honey. DC honey can be found in a rainbow of colors, from white to a dark maple-syrup-like color. When creating varietal honey (like orange blossom, lavender, buckwheat, etc.), beekeepers keep track of which flowers are blooming and then take the honey from the hive during that bloom to achieve a more concentrated flavor based on that one flower.

Through this project, they are hoping to create a plant list for different cities and urban areas which will indicate the plants that bees are foraging on and also highlight what could be planted in certain areas. Biodiversity not only improves the health of the honey bees but also helps the native pollinators and solitary bees. As we see more green rooftops and environmental initiatives in cities, this would be a perfect opportunity to collaborate and inform the choices that cities make in creating diverse habitats for pollinators.

For urban beekeeping endeavors to succeed, it is paramount that these hives are managed with routine care by well-trained beekeepers. Urban beekeeping companies like The Best Bees Company and Alvéole (a Montreal-based company) should partner with local beekeeping organizations in the cities where they set up their hives. Dialogue between local experts and new beekeepers will not only lead to better communication but, ultimately, a better environment for pollinators to thrive. We need to conserve and restore ecosystems to sustain the health and well-being of Earth's inhabitants. The interconnection among people, pollinators, and the broader environment is extremely valuable and I, for one, am thankful for these busy bees.

CHAPTER 9

Medicine from the Hive

"Just a spoonful of sugar honey..." is a phrase that I like to sing in my head as I swallow a teaspoon of honey as part of my nighttime routine. The healing properties of hive products have been studied for centuries, and I have been personally exploring the benefits over the last few years.

BEEKEEPER'S NATURALS

Carly Stein's business idea started with a sore throat. When she was studying abroad in Europe, she experienced a recurrence of tonsillitis that could have caused her to return to her home country of Canada for surgery. She stopped in to a local pharmacy in Florence, Italy and they recommended a propolis-infused treatment. She was cured of her golf-ball sized tonsils after less than a week and could not stop thinking about the effectiveness of this natural treatment as opposed to traditional antibiotics and other conventional options that she had tried when she was growing up.

Throughout her travels in Europe—from Copenhagen to Barcelona—she was able to find propolis, royal jelly, and pollen at corner stores. When she returned to Canada, she could not find propolis extract. She decided to apprentice with a local beekeeper to learn how to harvest propolis for herself. Carly used the chemistry lab at her college to create her own natural immune support spray with propolis. She then shared the spray with her friends, and they too experienced the healing benefits of propolis.

She could not shake this idea and experience of creating wellness products, even as she transitioned to a career in investment banking. Carly was working on the trading floor at Goldman Sachs, but she said she was miserable. She was extremely successful and, yet she was unhappy and depressed. In an interview with Chris Kresser, Carly said, "I sat down with myself because depression is not sustainable, and I made a spreadsheet about happiness and what I can do to get there and when I've been the happiest in my life. And the thing that I kept coming back to was working with the bees and making bee products" (Kresser 2018).

She decided to revisit the propolis-infused throat spray as a business idea which morphed into creating a wellness brand using hive-powered remedies. She wanted to make a difference in the world and Wall Street was not the place for her to make that happen. She first started selling her DIY products at farmers markets before deciding to go full-time with her endeavor. She quit her job (despite interventions from friends and family) and slept on her best friend's couch for six months, sacrificing and hustling to eventually launch what is now known as one of the most successful bee product companies: Beekeeper's Naturals. Carly said in an interview with the *Logician*, "I am so grateful that I persevered, trusted my gut, and created this wild career for myself" (Mirchevski 2019).

The company was founded in Canada in 2017 and has since expanded its footprint in the United States. Beekeeper's Naturals products can now be found on the shelves of Whole Foods, as well as selling direct-to-consumer through their online store. They sell honey infused with superfoods like bee pollen and propolis, as well as supplements created from hive products. The company is now a certified B-Corporation and Carly was listed in Forbes 30 under 30 US & Canada 2019 for Food & Drink. Beekeeper's Naturals propolis throat spray is one of the top cold and flu products on Amazon, and they raised over $700,000 from Wild Ventures and Thrive Market Ventures (Forbes 2019).

Carly's story is fascinating to me as someone interested in supporting bees while also using hive products for good in the world. Similar to Carly (who has arthritis and psoriasis), I also suffer from an autoimmune disease, Hashimoto's thyroiditis, and have often sought natural remedies where traditional Western medicine has failed to ease the symptoms. I have found that combining Western medicine (including my daily thyroid medication) with alternative therapies has improved my healing.

I have included honey bee hive products (honey, propolis, pollen, and royal jelly) as well as turmeric; raw fruit and vegetable juices; mushrooms like Lion's mane, Cordyceps, Reishi, Chaga, etc.; collagen; probiotics; and fermented foods into my wellness routine. Some medicines are filled with artificial ingredients and induce other negative side effects. For example, I was trying to find an alternative to nonsteroidal anti-inflammatory drugs (NSAIDs) like ibuprofen and naproxen sodium because they can cause damage to the gut lining. I have switched to turmeric and black pepper-based capsules which have been helpful to both alleviate any pain I have been feeling and to maintain good gut flora.

Beekeeper's Naturals aims to "reinvent the medicine cabinet." For example, the typical over-the-counter cough syrup uses corn syrup and artificial dyes to create the sweet flavor and red or purple coloring. Thanks to Beekeeper's Naturals, there is no longer the need to trade effectiveness for other negative side effects. Their cough syrup product contains buckwheat honey, elderberry fruit extract, bee propolis, and Chaga mushroom. It is free of artificial colors, fillers, alcohol, GMOs, and refined sugar.

The products are backed by scientific research and built on thousands of years of homemade recipes and remedies that have been passed down to subsequent generations. The natural world sustained human history for centuries before the advent of modern medicine. Beekeeper's Naturals taps into the healing properties of nature and transforms them into a consumer product that is affordable and available on a mass scale. Carly Stein is one among many people who are exploring the healing potential of bee products.

It is encouraging to me that honey, pollen, propolis, and royal jelly are being talked about in wider audiences, outside of the scientific and beekeeping communities. I am grateful that the wonder and magic of the bees are being brought to light in a new way for a new generation of consumers.

HONEY

Raw honey is one of the most delicious and surprisingly nutritious foods on the planet. It is packed with beneficial enzymes and easily digestible sugars. Honey can be used as a poultice and smeared on wounds for skin healing. It can also be used as a face mask to reduce inflammation.

As Carly explains, taking a spoonful of honey before bed can help with calming one down and inducing sleep due to the slow steady rise in insulin and the activation of serotonin and melatonin production in the brain (Kresser 2018). In studies of children with upper respiratory tract infections, honey relieved symptoms of nocturnal cough and sleep difficulty better than the placebo (silan date extract) (Cohen et al. 2012). In another study, adults with coronary issues experienced improved sleep quality after drinking a milk-honey mixture (Fakhr-Movahedi, Mirohammadkhani, Ramezani 2018).

Of course, I personally would recommend buying honey from your local area as a first step. Fortunately, I do not suffer from seasonal allergies, which local honey can help alleviate due to the presence of small doses of local plant material in the honey. However, it is to be noted that using local honey for allergies may come with risks, including anaphylaxis in people with severe allergies. Infants should also not consume honey as it can contain spores of the bacterium that causes botulism (Centers for Disease Control and Prevention 2019).

Chris Kresser, MS, LAc, a practitioner of integrative and functional medicine, has recommended raw honey for both upper respiratory problems and wound healing and staph infections on the skin (Kresser 2018). Chris discussed over-the-counter cough medicines with Carly on a 2018 episode of his podcast *Revolution Health Radio* (Kresser 2018). During their interview, Kresser said if he were posed the question, "If you could only choose two to four supplements or superfood kinds of products to take with you in a crisis situation, what would you choose?" he responded that honey would one of the four (Kresser 2018).

PROPOLIS

Propolis perhaps is one of the lesser-known hive products. The term "propolis" was coined by Aristotle from the Greek words *pro* (before) and *polis* (city), meaning before the city or defender of the city (Martinotti, Ranzato 2015). Ancient Egyptians, Persians, and Romans used propolis to alleviate ailments and act as an embalming substance. Bees collect plant and tree resins, and then the resins undergo an enzymatic process. The result is a sticky amber- or brown-colored substance. Bees use it as an anti-germ agent and often pack crevices and gaps in the hive to create a protective layer. They even line the front entrance of the hive and the cells with propolis to create the most sterile environment possible for their young and bees returning from foraging. Propolis is antioxidant-rich and used by bees to prevent the spread of germs and promote hygiene.

Propolis has over 300 beneficial compounds and is the active ingredient in Beekeeper's Naturals throat spray. Propolis "supports our immune systems, soothes scratchy throats, and helps combat free radical damage in the body" (Beekeeper's Naturals 2021). Free radical damage contributes to chronic health problems such as cardiovascular and inflammatory disease, cataracts, and cancer. A diet rich in antioxidants can help prevent the formation of radicals, as well as encouraging their decomposition (Lobo et al. 2010). Propolis is a true champion as it is anti-viral, anti-fungal, anti-microbial, anti-bacterial, and anti-inflammatory (Przybyłek, Karpiński 2019).

POLLEN

Bee pollen is another product that we do not necessarily think of as consumable, but it can be sprinkled on salads, on toast, or infused into smoothies. Consuming bee pollen is not recommended for those with pollen or bee allergies. Pollen is used by bees as a protein source. They collect and store it to complement the other nutrients they receive from nectar. Bee pollen is a ball or pellet of gathered flower pollen packed by honey bees. Bee pollen contains the whole pollen grain, outer shell included. Honey bee secretions create a fermentation process that breaks down the walls of the plant pollen grains and allows the nutrients to be more readily available.

Carly mentioned, "It contains nearly all nutrients required by humans, and it's really rich in protein...it's full of free-forming amino acids, vitamins including B-complex vitamins, which help with energy levels, and has folic acid. Bee pollen is kind of like an all-natural food-based bioavailable multivitamin" (Kresser 2018).

ROYAL JELLY

Royal jelly is a honey bee secretion that is produced by the heads of worker bees. It is composed of water, protein, simple sugars, fatty acids, a bio-active compound, as well as trace minerals. Royal jelly is one of the most amazing substances—it actually creates queens! Larvae that are fed royal jelly become queen bees. In the first three days of development, all bees are fed royal jelly. However, after the third day, worker bees and drones are fed a standard diet of pollen and honey. The queen will continue to be fed royal jelly. She grows longer and larger than the other bees. It makes sense that this substance would be rich in nutrients and antioxidants.

"Royal jelly offers nutrients and antioxidants that may support hormonal balance and brain health. Thanks to rare beneficial compounds, like 10-HAD, this substance may help improve cognition and fend off brain fog" (Beekeeper's Naturals 2021). On Kresser's podcast, Carly explained that when you combine raw honey with royal jelly, it becomes a source of Bifidobacteria. Propolis is a prebiotic. Therefore, if you have honey with royal jelly and propolis, you will have both a probiotic and a prebiotic (Kresser 2018). It is a good example of the bee products interacting together positively.

Royal jelly has been used in traditional Chinese medicine to boost fertility and balance hormones. It also has immune-boosting and immuno-modulatory properties.

Royal jelly is one of the only natural products to contain acetylcholine, which is used for "helping a healthy brain, for reducing your odds of neurodegenerative conditions, for brain healing, for focus, memory, concentration" (Kresser 2018). What is amazing about these products is that they are not just trying to effect a short-term change, but also a longer-term focus on holistic health. With all the evidence that bee products can be beneficial to our health, it is no wonder many companies are interested in creating new and effective products with these ingredients.

SWEETBIO

I was introduced to SweetBio through the Rural Opportunity Initiative Scholars Program at Georgetown University. As a member of the year-long program, I am lucky to hear guest speakers each week that discuss their companies and involvement in rural America. I learned about SweetBio through Innova Memphis, a pre-seed, seed, and early-stage investor focused on starting and funding high-growth companies in the biosciences, technology, and agricultural technology fields. SweetBio is one of the start-ups that Innova Memphis invested in.

SweetBio was founded by Kayla Rodriguez Graff and Isaac Rodriguez, a brother and sister team in Memphis, Tennessee. They focus on using medical-grade honey for wound care. They invented APIS®, a bioengineered wound product for the management of chronic and acute wounds. The product includes Manuka honey, which is said to inhibit bacteria growth and promote healing.

The company started by creating an innovative tool that could be used in guided tissue regeneration (GTR). GTR is a method used to repair periodontal defects to support and stabilize the tooth or teeth. Periodontal disease occurs when bacteria are trapped under the gums and leads to a chronic infection. GTR uses an artificial membrane to keep soft tissue from growing in the gaps between teeth and bone (Fairview Health Services). SweetBio first created a honey-infused product that could help in healing the mouth after oral surgery. Isaac first thought about the idea when he was working on his PhD in Biomedical Engineering at the University of Memphis (U of M). A clinician reached out to the U of M Biomedical Engineering lab seeking a better membrane for oral surgeries. Rodriguez then followed the "lean startup" philosophy of developing a product for a specific user.

SweetBio shifted the product away from the dental market to the wound care market due to increased potential for growth. The product has now been named APIS®, after *Apis mellifera* (the Latin name for honey bee) and is used to treat wounds such as diabetic ulcers, bedsores, and lesions at surgical sites. It is a patch that contains gelatin, manuka honey, and a nanoparticle called hydroxyapatite that helps tissue rebuild. The patch can be placed on a wound and will dissolve in a few days. In 2019, it was issued a US patent (co-assigned to the University of Memphis) for the technology, and the product was cleared by the FDA. In recent studies, it was shown to have reduced bacteria and inflammation during the wound healing process. The manuka honey in the product contains chemical compounds, including methylglyoxal (MGO) and Bee Defensin-1, which act as a natural antibiotic for healing (Oneal 2020).

While the patch is currently being sold to doctors and hospitals, they hope to sell APIS® directly to consumers in the future. They are working through the clinical trial phase now and are awaiting the results from these studies. "We are actually helping our loved ones heal", Kayla mentioned on *cityCurrent* radio (cityCurrent 2020). They are in the perfect place, as Memphis is the hub for medical device companies.

WOMEN FOUNDERS

The business for products derived from the hive is looking up. As Carly mentioned in an interview with *C-Suite Quarterly*, "Consumers are paying more attention now than ever to what's in their products, where they're getting them from, and how they impact their bodies...Customers are becoming more conscious of avoiding dirty chemicals and starting to prioritize sustainability and natural products" (C-Suite Quarterly 2020).

As women founders, Carly and Kayla have motivated me to consider an entrepreneurial journey, as well as the pursuit of my own personal wellness. Carly said in an interview with the *Logician*, "No matter how silly your business idea looks to the world, if you believe in it strongly enough, anything is possible. Stop being miserable by working a job you do not like, love, or appreciate, and go follow your dreams. Stop putting yourself through situations you do not want, just because the job is well-paid. Find what you believe in. Find what makes you happy" (Mirchevski 2019).

All my life, I have compared myself to others and often found myself struggling to find my path within traditional markers of success. I am learning to strive toward my dreams, and this book is one example of leaping into the unknown. I have let the fear of not being "enough" be the driver in my life for so long, but I am finally discovering what is possible beyond that lie. I can pursue my interests like gardening or creating art, even if those activities do not earn me any profit or become anything professional. I am worthy, regardless of the accomplishments on my resumé or how much money I have in the bank. I can be a businesswoman and a beekeeper, or anything in between.

Conclusion

You may ask, "What now?" after reading the stories contained in this book.

We are all connected—plants, animals, humans. The ecosystem is a vast, mysterious, and beautiful place. We need to take care of each other. I know this sounds like a desperate plea (and it partly is!), but I know how vital it is after spending hours in conversations with experts, doing research, and reflecting on my findings as I walked in the woods. I confirmed what I had thought would be true: our actions matter, even more than I would have previously imagined.

I have gratitude in my heart for those that shared their time and stories with me. Through their candor and openness, the crust of cynicism and skepticism about "does this matter?" was chipped away. My heart and mind were rejuvenated by my conversations. Perhaps my own life can change because of what I have learned, and maybe—just maybe—other people can benefit from this information too.

I do not claim that honey bees will change everyone's lives. I am also pretty adamant that not everyone should become a beekeeper. My hope is that this book can be a companion for people seeking to be in touch with the natural world, or who are interested in building community, or even for those who are simply looking to soak up the wisdom of resilient, innovative, and generous people.

Throughout this book-writing journey, I have come to deepen my admiration for the bees and those who care for them. We have experienced beekeeping through the eyes of incarcerated persons and returning citizens, veterans and first responders, rural farmers, urban dwellers, students, and many more.

The fiber that ties us all together is not a myth. By virtue of being a human on this planet, we are immersed in the environment.

We may not be aware that we exist in relation to the natural world if all we see is concrete and steel. Yet, even the most densely packed cities cannot elude nature—the wind still blows, the rain still pours, and the sun still shines. Weeds grow up between the cracks in the pavement. We can try to suppress it and fight it, but we are creatures in the natural world.

It is Friday afternoon and I have my windows open to let the breeze into my room. As I drink my tea with honey, I reflect on all that I have learned (and, oh, how much more I do not yet know!).

The connection we seek can be found, as long as we are willing to be open and vulnerable. The bees and their keepers have shown me that if we are quiet and listen to the rhythms of our world, we can nourish both it and ourselves—taking proper care of this space we inhabit. The dwelling place of tiny bees and mighty trees, and you and me.

If you are looking for a few practical steps you can incorporate into your daily life, may I suggest the following:

- patronize local beekeepers rather than buying bulk honey at box stores.
- advocate for legal beekeeping in your cities.
- use little to no pesticides in your gardening and landscaping.
- ditch the pristine grass-only lawn for one with a few weeds and wildflowers.
- plant native plants and trees in your yard to increase forage for pollinators.
- create a bee bath with water for bees to drink (make sure you add some stones, otherwise the bees will drown).
- buy or build native bee hotels and install them on your property.
- upload photos of native bees to "citizen scientist" apps.
- if you see a swarm, call your local beekeepers association to relocate them.
- attend agricultural fairs to introduce children to animals at an early age.
- donate money, time, and talent to pollinator organizations.

Resources

BEEKEEPER'S NATURALS

www.beekeepersnaturals.com
customercare@beekeepersnaturals.com
+1-844-503-4242

BEES FOR DEVELOPMENT

www.beesfordevelopment.org
info@beesfordevelopment.org
+44-16-0071-4848

BEES4VETS

www.bees4vets.org
beekeeper@bees4vets.org
+1-775-440-6111

THE BEST BEES COMPANY

www.bestbees.com

info@bestbees.com

+1-617-445-2322

DETROIT HIVES

www.detroithives.org

info@detroithives.org

+1-248-808-8467

EARTHBEAT SOLUTIONS FOUNDATION

www.earthbeatfoundation.org

connect@earthbeatfoundation.org

+49-16-3593-3105

GEORGETOWN UNIVERSITY BEE CAMPUS

www.stia.georgetown.edu/engagement/student-initiatives/
bee-campus

gucomm@georgetown.edu

+1-202-687-0100

HEROES TO HIVES

www.canr.msu.edu/veterans/veterans-programming/
heroes-to-hives

H2H@msu.edu

+1-517-355-1855

HIVES FOR HEROES

www.hivesforheroes.com

support@hivesforheroes.com

+1-713-391-9261

MISSION BEELIEVE

www.missionbeelieve.com

missionbeelieve@gmail.com

+1-727-804-5251

SUSTAINABILITY IN PRISONS PROJECT

www.sustainabilityinprisons.org

spp@evergreen.edu

+1-360-867-6863

SWEET BEGINNINGS

www.beelovebuzz.com

beelove@nlen.org

+1-773-638-7058

SWEETBIO

www.sweetbio.com

info@sweetbio.com

+1-540-424-9027

UNDER THE MANGO TREE SOCIETY

www.utmtsociety.org

info@utmtsociety.org

+91-22-4973-1965

UNIVERSITY OF MARYLAND BEE SQUAD

www.umdbeesquad.com

beesquad@umd.edu

+1-301-458-0640

THE XERCES SOCIETY FOR INVERTEBRATE CONSERVATION

www.xerces.org

pollinators@xerces.org

+1-855-232-6639

Acknowledgments

To Mom, Pop, and Connor—everything I do, I do for you. This book is one fruit of your love and encouragement for me and all my journeys in life.

To Fran, Rach, and Héloïse—I would not have survived this year (or the past fifteen!) without you. Your faces are the ones that remind me of who I am.

To my goddaughter Teddy—your joy is contagious, and time spent with you always revives my soul.

To my interviewees Adam Ingrao, Ginger and Daniel Fenwick, Kelli Bush, Mark Dykes, Monica Schmitt, Morgan Hill, Paige Mulhern, Shohei Morita, Steve Jimenez, and Sujana Krishnamoorthy—you are the life of these pages. Thank you for sharing your stories with me. It has been an honor to meet you and learn from you.

To the Creator Institute and New Degree Press team—for cultivating an environment that allowed my dream to become a reality.

To my editors Aislyn Gilbert and Morgan Rohde—for making my words shine brighter, and for allowing me the space to turn my thoughts into something beautiful.

To Richard and Rose—your thoughtful insights were instrumental in shaping the manuscript to be clearer without losing its heart.

To my friends, family, and community of supporters—my deepest gratitude to you, from my hometown in Mendham, to my university home in Montreal, to my current home of Washington, DC, and beyond. This book would not exist without your generous contributions.

Appendix

INTRODUCTION

Collins, Sonya. "The Loneliness Epidemic Has Very Real Consequences." *WebMD*. November 29, 2019. https://www.webmd.com/balance/features/loneliness-epidemic-consequences.

Cook, Gareth. "Why We Are Wired to Connect." *Scientific American*. October 22, 2013. https://www.scientificamerican.com/article/why-we-are-wired-to-connect/.

The National Aeronautics and Space Administration (NASA). "Climate Change: How Do We Know?" June 2, 2021. https://climate.nasa.gov/evidence/.

CHAPTER 1

Cooke, Lucy. *The Truth About Animals: Stoned Sloths, Lovelorn Hippos, and Other Tales from the Wild Side of Wildlife.* Basic Books, 2018: 1-2, 268.

Foster, Craig. *My Octopus Teacher.* Directed by Pippa Ehrlich and James Reed. South Africa: A Netflix Original Documentary. September 7, 2020.

CHAPTER 2

Merriam-Webster.com Dictionary, s.v. "colony collapse disorder," accessed May 5, 2021, https://www.merriam-webster.com/dictionary/colony%20collapse%20disorder.

Moritz, Robin F.A. and Silvio Erler. "Lost Colonies Found in a Data Mine: Global Honey Trade but Not Pests or Pesticides as a Major Cause of Regional Honeybee Colony Declines." *Agriculture, Ecosystems & Environment* Volume 216 (2016): 44-50, https://doi.org/10.1016/j.agee.2015.09.027.

CHAPTER 3

Frazier, Maryann. "Beekeeping Basics." Pennsylvania State Extension Publications, 2004.

Godin, Mélissa. "The Bee Whisperers of Slovenia Have a Plan to Save Colonies From Climate Change." *Time.* May 6, 2020. https://time.com/5815141/slovenia-bees-climate-change/.

Kasiotis, Konstantinos M., Chris Anagnostopoulos, Pelagia Anastasiadou, and Kyriaki Machera. "Pesticide Residues in

Honeybees, Honey and Bee Pollen by LC-MS/MS Screening: Reported Death Incidents in Honeybees." *Science of the Total Environment.* 2014 Jul 1; 485-486:633-642. doi: 10.1016/j. scitotenv.2014.03.042.

Mullin, Christopher A., Maryann Frazier, James L. Frazier, Sara Ashcraft, Roger Simonds, Dennis vanEngelsdorp, and Jeffery S. Pettis. "High Levels of Miticides and Agrochemicals in North American Apiaries: Implications for Honey Bee Health." *PLOS ONE* 5(3): e9754. https://doi.org/10.1371/journal. pone.0009754.

Otis, Gard. "Honey bees — the canary in the coal mine: Gard Otis at TEDxGuelphU." Filmed November 2013 at the University of Guelph in Guelph, Ontario. TED video, 23:38. https://www. youtube.com/watch?v=SYPP7vBxGFs.

United States Department of Agriculture (USDA). "Conservation Reserve Program, Honey Bee Habitat Initiative." 2017.

Wilfert, L., G. Long, H.C. Leggett, P. Schmid-Hempel, R. Butlin, S. J. M. Martin, and M. Boots. "Deformed Wing Virus in a Recent Global Epidemic in Honeybees Driven by Varroa Mites." *Science* 351, 6273 (2016): 594-597. doi: 10.1126/science. aac9976.

Xerces Society. "How Neonicotinoids Can Kill Bees: The Science Behind the Role These Insecticides Play in Harming Bees." 2nd Edition. 2016. https://xerces.org/ publications/scientific-reports/how-neonicotinoids-can-kill-bees.

Xerces Society. "Invertebrate Conservation Fact Sheet: Nests for Native Bees." May 2018. https://www.xerces.org/publications/fact-sheets/nests-for-native-bees.

CHAPTER 4

Barber, Brenda. "Building Confidence, Restoring Self-Worth." May 21, 2020. In *Inside Sweet Beginnings*. Podcast, MP3 Audio. https://blog.beelovebuzz.com/insidesb-episode2/.

Bureau of Justice Statistics. Corrections Statistical Analysis Tool (CSAT) Prisoners Quick Tables, "Sentenced prisoners under the jurisdiction of state or federal correctional authorities, December 31, 1978-2016." https://www.bjs.gov/nps/resources/documents/QT_total%20jurisdiction%20count_total.xlsx.

Bureau of Justice Statistics. Historical Statistics on Prisoners in State and Federal Institutions, Year end 1925-86, Table 3. https://www.bjs.gov/content/pub/pdf/hspsfiy25-86.pdf#page=17.

Couloute, Lucius. "Nowhere to Go: Homelessness among Formerly Incarcerated People." Prison Policy. August 2018. https://www.prisonpolicy.org/reports/housing.html.

Couloute, Lucius and Daniel Kopf. "Out of Prison & Out of Work: Unemployment among formerly incarcerated people." Prison Policy. July 2018. https://www.prisonpolicy.org/reports/outofwork.html.

Davis, Lois M. and Jennifer L. Steele, Robert Bozick, Malcolm V. Williams, Susan Turner, Jeremy N. V. Miles, Jessica Saunders, and Paul S. Steinberg. *How Effective Is Correctional Education and Where Do We Go from Here?: The Results of a Comprehensive Education.* Rand Corporation: 2014.

Erisman, Wendy and Jeanne Bayer Contardo. *Learning to Reduce Recidivism: A 50-State Analysis of Postsecondary Correctional Education Policy.* The Institute for Higher Education Policy: November 2005.

North Lawndale Employment Network. "Program Methodologies." 2008. https://www.issuelab.org/resources/6004/6004.pdf.

Roberts Enterprise Development Fund (REDF). "Sweet Beginnings - Creating a Buzz in Chicago." December 7, 2017. Video, 4:02. https://www.youtube.com/watch?v=wGOlPeIQZOE.

Sustainability in Prisons Project. "What SPP Is and Isn't." http:// sustainabilityinprisons.org/about/what-spp-is-and-isnt.

The Marshall Project. "A State-by-State Look at Coronavirus in Prisons." https://www.themarshallproject.org/2020/05/01/ a-state-by-state-look-at-coronavirus-in-prisons.

The United States Department of Justice, National Institute of Corrections (NICIC), Washington State, "2018 National Averages." https://nicic.gov/state-statistics/2018/washington-2018.

University of California San Francisco. "For Prisoners, Pandemic Hits with Greater Force." Kurtzman, Laura. October 25, 2020. https://www.ucsf.edu/news/2020/10/418876/prisoners-pandemic-hits-greater-force.

CHAPTER 5

Carter, Josh. "You Can Learn a Lot from a Bee." September 8, 2020. In *Veteran Founder Podcast*. Podcast, MP3 Audio. https://www. iheart.com/podcast/256-veteran-founder-podcast-43087634/ episode/75-you-can-learn-a-lot-71218851.

Casey, Michael and Mike Householder. "Veterans with PTSD, Anxiety Turn to Beekeeping for Relief." *Military Times.* September 11, 2019. https://www.militarytimes.com/education-transition/2019/09/11/veterans-with-ptsd-anxiety-turn-to-beekeeping-for-relief.

McArthur, Claire. "Bugs for Change: Nonprofit Brings Beekeeping to Vets Suffering from PTSD." *Edible Reno-Tahoe.* Spring 2020. https://ediblerenotahoe.com/magazine/bees-4-vets.

Quick, Walter Jacob. "Bee Keeping. April 1919. To the Disabled Soldiers, Sailors, and Marines. To Aid Them in Choosing a Vocation." Government Printing Office. 1919.

United States Census Bureau, Veterans. 2019.

United States Census Bureau, Veterans. 2020.

United States Department of Veterans Affairs. "2020 National Veteran Suicide Prevention Annual Report." 2020. https://www. mentalhealth.va.gov/docs/data-sheets/2020/2020-National-Veteran-Suicide-Prevention-Annual-Report-11-2020-508.pdf.

United States Department of Veterans Affairs. "Veterans Employment Toolkit." September 2, 2015. https://www.va.gov/ vetsinworkplace/docs/em_challengesreadjust.asp.

CHAPTER 6

Bees for Development. "Beekeeping for Landless People." January 19, 2021. https://beesfordevelopment.org/article/beekeeping-for-landless-young-people/?mc_cid=698900125a&mc_eid=bcb10738db.

Bees for Development. "Beekeeping Training Project in Ethiopia Brings Relief in the Time of COVID." May 13, 2021. https://beesfordevelopment.org/article/beekeeping-training-project-in-ethiopia-brings-relief-in-the-time-of-covid/?mc_cid=698900125a&mc_eid=bcb10738db.

Bees for Development. Number 138, April 2021. https://issuu.com/beesfd/docs/bfdj_138_-__150_dpi_rgb_final_26-04-21?mc_cid=698900125a&mc_eid=bcb10738db.

Earthbeat Solutions Foundation. "HEARTBEAT HONEY - Bee Keeping as an Alternative to Gold Mining!" January 4, 2018. Video, 4:00. https://www.youtube.com/watch?v=sRkai7crpKI.

Elson, Jim. "Liquid Gold." October 1, 2018. Video, 15:32. https://vimeo.com/292648446.

Food and Agriculture Organization of the United Nations. "Beekeeping Helps to Create Sustainable Livelihoods." http://www.fao.org/3/y5110e/y5110e02.htm.

Monks, Kieron. "The High Price of Uganda's Gold Rush." CNN. January 3, 2018. https://www.cnn.com/2017/06/12/africa/uganda-mining-corruption/index.html.

Our Story, Bees for Development, https://beesfordevelopment.org/about-us/our-story/.

Our Story, Under The Mango Tree, https://www.utmt.in/pages/our-story.

Patel, Vidushi, Natasha Pauli, Eloise Biggs, Liz Barbour, and Brian Boruff. "Why Bees Are Critical for Achieving Sustainable Development." *Ambio* 50, 49-59 (2021): https://link.springer.com/article/10.1007/s13280-020-01333-9.

The 17 Sustainable Development Goals, The United Nations, https://sdgs.un.org/goals.

CHAPTER 7

Angelova, Kamelia. "Bleak Photos Capture the Fall of Detroit." *Business Insider.* October 2, 2012. https://www.businessinsider.com/the-incredible-decline-of-detroit-photos-2012-10.

Detroit Hives Instagram, https://www.instagram.com/detroithives/.

Encyclopedia of Detroit, Detroit Historical Society, https://detroithistorical.org/learn/encyclopedia-of-detroit/flag-detroit.

National Geographic. "Detroit's Urban Beekeepers are Transforming the City's Vacant Lots | Short Film Showcase." June 24, 2019. Video, 5:58. https://www.youtube.com/watch?v=h_2GMByKxNQ.

CHAPTER 8

Bee Campus USA. "Bee Campus USA Commitments." Xerces Society. https://beecityusa.org/bee-campus-usa-commitments/.

Bee City USA. "Bee City USA Commitments." Xerces Society. https://beecityusa.org/bee-city-usa-commitments/.

National Geographic, "A Dollop of Sweet Science." February 6, 2018. https://www.nationalgeographic.com/magazine/graphics/a-dollop-of-sweet-science.

NowThis Earth. "Why Bees Thrive in Cities | One Small Step | NowThis Earth." October 19, 2020. Video, 10:40. https://www.youtube.com/watch?v=lY9VwVx5DSU.

Obama, Barack. Presidential Memorandum, "Creating a Federal Strategy to Promote the Health of Honey Bees and Other Pollinators." The White House. June 20, 2014. https://obamawhitehouse.archives.gov/the-press-office/2014/06/20/presidential-memorandum-creating-federal-strategy-promote-health-honey-b.

CHAPTER 9

Beekeeper's Naturals. "Ingredients." 2021. https://beekeepersnaturals.com/pages/ingredients.

Centers for Disease Control and Prevention. "Botulism Prevention." Last reviewed June 7, 2019. https://www.cdc.gov/botulism/prevention.html.

cityCurrent. "SweetBio: Honey Incorporated Materials for Wound Care." October 11, 2020. *In Memphis Radio Show*. Radio, MP3 audio, 15:46. https://citycurrent.news/2020/10/11/sweetbio-honey-incorporated-materials-for-wound-care.

Cohen HA, J Rozen, H Kristal, Y Laks, M Berkovitch, Y Uziel, E Kozer, A Pomeranz, and H Efrat. "Effect of Honey on Nocturnal Cough and Sleep Quality: A Double-Blind, Randomized, Placebo-Controlled Study." *Pediatrics* 130(3), (2012): 465-71. doi: 10.1542/peds.2011-3075.

C-Suite Quarterly. "Carly Stein: How the Founder of Beekeeper's Naturals is Revolutionizing the Wellness Industry." April 27, 2020. https://csq.com/2020/04/carly-stein-how-the-founder-of-beekeepers-naturals-is-revolutionizing-the-wellness-industry.

Fairview Health Services. "Periodontal Disease: Guided Tissue Regeneration (GTR)." https://www.fairview.org/Patient-Education/Articles/English/p/e/r/i/o/Periodontal_Disease_Guided_Tissue_Regeneration_GTR_40015.

Fakhr-Movahedi Ali, Mirmohammadkhani Majid, and Ramezani Hossein. "Effect of Milk-Honey Mixture on the Sleep Quality of Coronary Patients: A Clinical Trial Study." *Clinical Nutrition ESPEN* 28, (2018): 132-135. https://doi.org/10.1016/j.clnesp.2018.08.015.

Forbes. "2019 30 Under 30 - Food & Drink." https://www.forbes.com/profile/carly-stein/?sh=526ffd88645c.

Kresser, Chris. "The Health Benefits of Bee Products, with Carly Stein." December 11, 2018. In Revolution Health Radio. Podcast, MP3 audio, 54.50. https://chriskresser.com/the-health-benefits-of-bee-products-with-carly-stein.

Lobo, V., A. Patil, A. Phatak, and N. Chandra. "Free Radicals, Antioxidants and Functional Foods: Impact on Human Health." *Pharmacognosy Review* 4, (2010): 118-126. doi:10.4103/0973-7847.70902.

Martinotti, Simona and Elia Ranzato. "Propolis: A New Frontier for Wound Healing?" *Burns & Trauma* 3, 9 (2015). https://doi.org/10.1186/s41038-015-0010-z.

Mirchevski, Bruno. "An Interview with Carly Stein, *Forbes* (US & Canada 2019) Food & Drink." April 3, 2019. Medium. https://medium.com/the-logician/an-interview-with-carly-stein-entrepreneur-4f7773bb61fe.

Oneal, Sheri. "Meet Sweetbio: The Memphis Startup for Advanced Honey-Based Wound Care." Launch Engine. December 4, 2020. https://launchengine.io/meet-sweetbio-the-memphis-startup-for-advanced-honey-based-wound-care/.

Phillips, Cristy. "Brain-Derived Neurotrophic Factor, Depression, and Physical Activity: Making the Neuroplastic Connection." *Neural Plasticity* 2017 (2017): 7260130. doi:10.1155/2017/7260130.

Przybyłek, Izabela and Tomasz M. Karpiński. "Antibacterial Properties of Propolis." *Molecules* 24, 11: 2047. (2019) doi:10.3390/molecules24112047.